PSYCHIATRY - THEORY, APPLICATIONS AND TREATMENTS

STORIES FROM THE BORDER

REFLECTIONS ON WAYS OF WORKING WITH PEOPLE WITH BORDERLINE PERSONALITY DISORDER LIVING IN THE COMMUNITY

Psychiatry - Theory, Applications and Treatments

Additional books in this series can be found on Nova's website
under the Series tab.

Additional e-books in this series can be found on Nova's website
under the e-book tab.

PSYCHIATRY - THEORY, APPLICATIONS AND TREATMENTS

STORIES FROM THE BORDER

REFLECTIONS ON WAYS OF WORKING WITH PEOPLE WITH BORDERLINE PERSONALITY DISORDER LIVING IN THE COMMUNITY

JOHN LITTLE
AND
DUNCAN THOMSON

nova publishers
New York

Library of Congress Cataloging-in-Publication Data

ISBN: 978-1-63321-916-8

Library of Congress Control Number: 2014951980

Published by Nova Science Publishers, Inc. † New York

To Marg, with thanks

Contents

PREFACE

This is a startlingly frank account of a psychiatrist's and a psychologist's learnings, milestones and mistakes when working with people with the characteristics of borderline personality disorder (BPD). The book is an examination of the physician and therapist as much as it is of this often 'alarming and bewildering' group of people.

Throughout their illuminating, frank and often moving accounts of their work, Doctors Little and Thomson elucidate and reflect on the principles that inform their practice and the practice of their mental health team colleagues. Importantly, the book also presents stories in their own words from the people with whom they all work. These stories offer further valuable insight into the experience of BPD and its treatment and therapy.

ACKNOWLEDGMENTS

Anyone who writes a book knows how long it takes. This has been a 12-month commitment in both our personal and professional lives. As such, we genuinely want to thank our families. Duncan has a young family, and his father questioned whether he should add on an extra job to his busy private and public practice. I'm (John) glad he did! Our thanks, then, to Nichola, William and Ben. My wife, Marg, helped me with all my writing, often despairing at my sloppiness! I have been genuinely touched that each of our children wanted to read an earlier book written on my time working in Bowman, a low secure unit in Cornwall, which led, in part, to this current book. It was my son Alex who suggested that it might be useful to get an editor with respect to this second project, and what a great idea that turned out to be.

I met Harry Ricketts at a busy coffee shop in Wellington, neither of us knowing what the other looked like. His kindness and generosity as he gently made thoughtful suggestions prompted us to write a second draft with a focus on an intelligent readership rather than trying to combine this with a technical audience. Although tempted, he had promised his wife not to take on another project! What he did, though, was find and put us in contact with Paula Wagemaker.

Living in the Maniototo region of New Zealand's South Island, she had enormous publishing experience, was available and more importantly was herself interested in the topic area. This time both Duncan and I met her in a coffee shop in Wellington. Paula had emailed us to say that she would have her pink phone on the table so that we could find her. I wrote back and said that I looked like a psychiatrist—beard and glasses! Duncan spotted her, and we sat down and went through the second draft together. Part of us wanted Paula to take over and do everything. But a part of us also wanted to learn something of her craft for ourselves in case we had to spend another year writing! Either way, this work would not have been possible without Paula. She has crafted our stories beautifully, and we remain extraordinarily grateful. As Duncan quipped, she makes us look positively clever!

Some of our writing and thinking has occurred in work-time, between patients or during CME (continuing medical education) time. At the risk of leaving out important people who have helped us along the way, we each want to thank particular people by name. We thank David Lobb in the UK, along with Janice Rouhan, Peter Blackman and Shane Murphy as well as Professor Norman James, who introduced me to Dawson and MacMillan's book while I was working in Australia. Particularly sincere thanks are extended to the Kapiti team where we both currently work. This project would not be possible without the support of Rosie Edwards, our clinical director, and Iain Barnes, our team leader. Their experience and level-headedness always lead us back in times of crisis.

Iain enabled us to gain the support of the clinic's administrative team for this project. Under Dale Brown's leadership, both she and Melina Chan covered while Heather Dryburgh typed, re-typed and re-typed, deleting already typed sections with the same good humour. Duncan and I continue to work at Kapiti because of this team, starting at the front desk with Admin, and also including our community psychiatric nurses Ruth, Rachael, Kate, David and Gerard, and occupational therapist, Sorcha Odgers. We also extend thanks and appreciation to Jen, Mon and Peter from Pathways for their warmth, humanity and commitment.

It seems peculiar to write 'and finally, our patients'. This book would never have been possible without your generosity and willingness to share your stories for others. We want to thank those of you whom we met in the UK and in Australia, and whom we'll probably never meet again. We hope if you ever read this that you recognize your part in shaping our practice and in teaching what we have tried to put to paper. We also hope that one or two of you whom we haven't written about or named know who you are and that you remain important influences in our professional lives. We especially thank those of you who wrote specifically for this book. Your, stories, comments and thoughts have made a contribution that is honest and revealing in ways that we could never capture. Thank you again.

Dr John Little and Dr Duncan Thomson
2014

About Us

Our team works in a small, unremarkable community health centre. The front of the building is a general medical outpatient facility for visiting specialists; Mental Health is tucked around the back. The location, semi-rural New Zealand, with a catchment population of about 40,000 people, could easily be in Australia or the UK, where we've worked. There is one psychiatrist, myself (John), and a part-time psychologist, Duncan, who is also co-author of this book. Team leader Iain works alongside our aforementioned five community psychiatric nurses, who are employed in various combinations of full-time and part-time work. We also have a part-time occupational therapist, Sorcha, a job-sharing administrative staff (Heather, Dale and Melina), and trainee registrars, psychologists, and nurses on clinical placements. We meet weekly, sometimes to grapple with the mind-numbing but inescapable service-required demands; often to engage in vigorous and robust debate about one of our clients who, along with us, is struggling with therapy.

When we were first invited to write this book, we excitedly sent off an outline of what it might look like and who might be involved. The publisher, Nova Science, replied swiftly, requesting a draft chapter; perhaps they were a little uncertain about the story-telling genre we wanted to adopt. Again, we aimed to reply promptly—to emphasise our interest and our ability to meet timelines. But we didn't manage this, partly because we needed time to discuss the project with the people we wanted to write about. We also needed to carefully choose who might illustrate the particular points we wanted to make and then asked them for their consent to include their story in the book.

Two other developments also delayed us. First, we'd begun to realise we were frightened of being looked on as experts. And when we're unsure, we wait, watch and reflect. The people we wanted to write about felt privileged. Jade, for example, wanted us to tell her story and wanted us to use her own name—she wanted people to *understand* her experience. We were humbled by the generosity of people such as Jade who suffer. We wanted to honour them by telling their stories as best we could. The second development also related to Jade. Whatever we were doing in our work with her seemed to have an effect, and when we tried it with other people, it appeared to work again. The pattern was not consistent, but it was clear enough to keep us going and to keep watching, refining our approach as we went along.

Our work emerges from the 'borders', from small numbers of patients, and from something that could easily be dismissed as having occurred by chance or by extraneous influences in each person's life. Nevertheless, we also sensed that what we were doing was making a difference; that we could present our thinking and practice in a book. We negotiated a new submission date with the publisher, and picked up our pens once more.

Heather had been typing and retyping our handwritten drafts, adding little bits at the bottom of various sections: 'I don't think this makes much sense. This doesn't make any sense! Expand. Delete.' When I finally decided to try to organize all of the material we'd produced, I placed the stapled chapters in order and covered the floor with them, like a mosaic. I'm not sure whether it was as much for my peace of mind or Heather's, but I gathered the pages together, went out, and showed her what we'd done so far. I wanted to assure her that although, as she'd made clear in her forthright but generous manner, the writing had started off on the rough side, it was coming together. 'Writing's a bit like *pounamu*' (New Zealand jade), I said to her after she'd looked through this new draft. 'It starts off as a piece of rock on the riverbed, but with cutting and polishing, it becomes shaped and smooth.' She looked at me: 'A bit more cutting and polishing, John!'

Buoyed, nonetheless, I went back to my room and worked out how many weeks were left before we had to submit the book to the publisher. Panic! But I still was uncertain as to how to present everything we'd written to date so that someone would want to read our book—and keep reading it. Duncan was out, so I asked David and Ruth what they'd want to read in a book on people with borderline personality disorder (BPD). Ruth smiled: 'The answer!'

Our ensuing discussion led to consideration of what our work situation had been like two to three years earlier. 'The day used to fall off from the fax machine each morning,' David recalled in his Welsh accent. 'Contacts would be faxed through overnight, and each morning we'd pick them up. One of us would rush off down the road to the local hospital, where one of our patients had been admitted during the night—again.' Ruth added, 'Thinking about, let alone talking about, doing it differently, was too frightening. Somehow we just got used to doing it this way and just kept doing it.'

As we continued talking, we began thinking about the people who had been, but were no longer, in our service, instead living their lives in the community. Ruth agreed that she'd find vignettes about them interesting, especially as they'd help her identify with the people we were describing, even though she hadn't met many of them. However, she concluded that once read, she'd probably not reread them, so what she wanted us to include as well was the theoretical underpinnings of our work.

Her comments were most helpful, especially as they helped us realise that our difficulty lay with deciding whether to write for a technical audience or for an intelligent general audience, or both. We agreed that it should be the latter. However, despite pitching the book at this audience, we considered we'd still provide material of interest and use to the former.

So here it is—a book about working with people predominantly with BPD who are living in the community. While we hesitate to provide an encompassing definition of BPD (Ruth's 'the answer' comment above implies why), the literature and our experience indicates that it is characterised by people, who, believing that they are fundamentally despicable, are exquisitely sensitive to rejection and abandonment. They have genuine difficulty managing the accompanying and abruptly changing moods and, in their stead, show their distress through deliberate self-harm and, sadly, occasionally through suicide. Given what has happened in their lives, and what the person has had to do in order to survive, it is of little surprise that they have no clear sense of who they are, instead experiencing at times a range of phenomena that, when presenting to services, are seen as 'alarming and bewildering'.[1] Our own record-keeping and discussion with colleagues elsewhere indicates that approximately 70 percent of people exhibiting these characteristics are women, and that, of these women, 70 percent experienced some form of sexual abuse during their formative years.

The stories in each chapter might take the form of a montage, fragments of information about people whom we met a long time ago, in another country. They might be about the same person, with whom we've travelled a long walk together. They might be stories from our own lives, or present our own thoughts and feelings as we observe how all of the above has added to or subtracted from our work.

Throughout, we discuss the theory informing what we do and at the end offer an annotated bibliography for those of you wanting to read a little more. But let's begin with a story that is about none of these yet is pertinent to all that we want to say in this book. It comes from China and features an elderly woman and two large pots.

A Gift to You

An elderly Chinese woman had two large pots, each hung on the end of a pole, which she carried across her neck. One of the pots had a crack in it while the other pot was perfect and always delivered a full portion of water. By the end of her long walks from the stream to the house, the cracked pot arrived only half full.

Day after day, the woman brought home only one and a half pots of water. The perfect pot was proud of its accomplishment. But the poor, cracked pot, ashamed of its imperfection, was miserable that it could only do half of what it had been made to do. After two years of what it perceived to be its bitter failure, the pot spoke to the woman one day by the stream. 'I am ashamed of myself, because this crack in my side causes water to leak out all the way back to your house.'

The old woman smiled: 'Did you notice that there are flowers on your side of the path, but not on the other pot's side? That's because I have always known about your flaw, so I planted flower seeds on your side of the path, and every day while we walk back, you water them. For two years, I have been able to pick these beautiful flowers to decorate the table. Without you being just the way you are, there would not be this beauty to grace the house.'

Part One: Taking Time

They always say time changes things, but you actually have to change them yourself—
Andy Warhol

Chapter 1

GETTING THE TIMING RIGHT BY SLOWING THINGS DOWN

Time is nature's way of making sure that everything doesn't happen at once—
Anon

The people who present to us with the characteristics of borderline personality disorder (BPD) all have stories to tell. But the telling of those stories takes time, which is not surprising given that they've usually been years in the making. They rarely understand their stories sufficiently well to be able to narrate them immediately let alone coherently. Their current behaviours, often destructive of themselves and others close to them, can be seen as evidence of them trying to make sense of or manage their stories, which generally begin with some form of trauma during childhood and adolescence. People need time not only to pull together the pieces of their stories but also to understand why and how those stories are affecting them. We, who strive to support them, need time to gain the same understandings so that we can decide on how we can help them make sense of their stories and begin to heal.

The stories in this chapter and subsequent commentary on them serve as an introduction to why and how we formulated our take time approach and its associated practice-related principles, which we detail in subsequent chapters. Each story holds within it the genesis of one or more of the threads of understanding of BPD we have gained over the years. This understanding, aided by discussion with colleagues, reference to the literature and the willingness of people to have their stories told and for us to reflect on them, has allowed us, *with time*, to weave those threads into our own stories of how we now work with people with BPD who are living in the community.

THE GENESIS OF AN IDEA

'I don't care anymore ...'

Monday morning, 8.30. Eva sits heavily. Her hair, which has long outgrown its garish colouring, is hastily tied back. The state of her clothing, her whole manner, speaks of her lost self-respect. She's given up; her voice has not: 'I dunno!' She defies yet another gentle attempt that might enable her to understand why she's feeling so miserable.

Weeks go by with little difference in the pattern of our meetings before I finally ask someone else to see her. I vaguely recall reading somewhere that referral is the point of maximal dishonesty. I've been dishonest with her. She's struggling, trying to survive the best way she knows how. But I can't help without her involvement and acknowledgement of her problems. I feel resentful and then guilty for being callous.

'I need looking after!'

Pat's relationship has just ended, and she's agreed with her friend that what she needs is time in hospital, which is where she'd gone when an earlier relationship ended. She arrives with her bags packed, keen to be admitted. She definitely doesn't want to talk to me, the psychiatrist. Eventually, she realises it's simpler to acquiesce, to have this chat with me, preparatory to it being continued tomorrow.

When our team sees Pat the next day, she's visibly different—relaxed, calm, pleasant. The inpatient staff note how well she's slept, how easily she interacts with everyone, and they're actually quite surprised she is even there. We wonder with her what this shift in mood might be about. Immediately, the hardness returns. Her arms cross. Her speech is abrupt. 'Yeah,' she says, 'it's all my fault!'

I ask her if she'd like to try to understand why her mood keeps changing so quickly. She responds by retreating to the need for medication. Last night, she was manic, she says; she therefore needs me to review her medicines. But then she does an about-turn, threatening to stop taking all her medicines and to stop eating and drinking. Despite her earlier admonition, our attempts to explore what medication might do for her are dismissed.

It's clear to us that this volatility will see Pat continuing to struggle, especially given the inevitable effect this behavioural pattern is having on her relationships. But the only way we can determine how we might help requires a place to talk, feel, explore—a place where we and Pat can try to make sense of how Pat's early life is continuing to affect her adult life.

'I keep coming here, but ...'

Ness is 18, but her dress and demeanour suggest she is younger. She sits sweetly in reception and giggles. Perhaps because of her apparent sweetness and an opportunity to intervene early, a residential therapeutic community in a private hospital had earlier offered her a place, and Ness had accepted. Some members of the hospital-based team I'm part of were outraged when this happened. She'd rarely attended appointments at our outpatients' clinic, and when she did, she chatted inconsequentially. Why, they asked, should she have this opportunity when others miss out? As a group, we'd talked in an attempt to reconcile differences in opinion about people like Ness who present with the characteristics of BPD. Some practitioners, for example, dispute such people are ill and because of this do not qualify for mental health services' support.

Some months later, the private hospital discharged Ness. Her behaviour had escalated to a point where she was acting out in ways that unsettled the work of their clinic. It appears to us that Ness had not been ready to engage in the healing process. Before the private hospital offered to admit her, our wish to help and her sweetness had led us to overlook her own lack of curiosity as to why she'd repeatedly arrived at our clinic door and, despite her time in hospital, was still doing so.

'I need to see you ... but then I don't'

Once again, Tom hasn't kept his appointment, and once again his aunt phones to rebook this latest missed session. Eventually, he does keep a scheduled appointment, says, 'Yep, DBT,[1] that sounds like what I need,' and then fails to keep the next appointment.

His aunt calls to say he's suicidal again—that he really needs to see us urgently. However, Tom typically doesn't turn up. We frantically try to find him only to learn that he's just met up with a friend and caught the bus into town. 'Chill man!' he quips when we do find him. Friends and family are worried too. But that's not enough. We need him to sign up and get involved—to recognise a problem and so start his journey towards mental health.

'I don't want to talk, let alone engage'

The first time I see Jess, she is curled up on a hospital bed in Casualty. She looks utterly miserable and alone. The staff make little effort to hide their contempt for her. She is wasting their time with this latest overdose. In their fatigue, they project this dissatisfaction onto her mental health team.

Jess is already well known to local mental health services. Gradually, almost methodically, her incidences of self-harm have been increasing. Even before meeting her, I knew of her and sensed she would be referred to me. I bask in the anticipated collegial approbation of being able to engage with, treat and cure this difficult patient. As expected, the day comes when a nurse and I are dispatched to the hospital to bring her home.

The nurse approaches her bed. Like a mother reassuring a scared infant, she acknowledges things are really hard for Jess, and does she feel like returning to her home with us? I'm struck by my reluctance to join in, instead simply introducing myself in a matter-of-fact tone. After a lengthy cajoling from the nurse, Jess nods her head a fraction: yes, she will allow us to take her home.

The journey in the car continues in a similar vein. My efforts at small-talk, big-talk, any talk are rejected, and I lapse into silence, accepting my role as chauffeur. I realise I appear crabby, judgemental and intolerant of her distress. Yet it does speak volumes of how Jess is interacting with us. For me, our humanness with patients is paramount; to be moved when what they are describing is particularly emotive and, moreover, to be prepared to admit this. However, despite Jess's obvious distress and my acknowledgement of it, she is not willing to let me be a part of it. She's unable to share the private experiences that might allow us to put her jigsaw together, to make sense of what has been happening in her life and to help her move beyond her distress.

[1] Dialectical behaviour therapy, a therapy designed to help people change ineffective and destructive behavioural patterns.

I am unsurprised, two weeks later, to find that when I formally assess Jess's suitability for the DBT programme, engaging with her remains difficult. She mumbles, head down, never looking at me and giving minimal detail in response to my increasingly exasperated line of questioning. Each time I point out to her that we cannot *hope* to address a problem that we do not jointly understand, she throws me a crumb of information that I greedily leap upon to assuage my guilt at being so direct with someone apparently so vulnerable. I have come into my session with her having no information whatsoever about her inner experience. I leave, none the wiser. Subsequent attempts to communicate to her what she needs to face, despite whatever fears plague her, so that she can work on her difficulties in a meaningful way, fail. My rescue fantasy dashed, I decide I cannot work with her on this basis.

A year on, Jess remains on the periphery of our service, having been passed from clinician to clinician, all of whom experience a degree of burnout directly commensurate with their attempts to help. Her behaviour has become increasingly dysfunctional, with a 'psychotic' presentation and overdoses of increasing severity. I can honestly say we understand her almost as poorly as we did when we first met her. But I would still like to help her rescue herself.

'I'm trying to understand'

Stephanie, or Steph as she prefers to call herself, is 43. She says she's been sent to me by a physician who reviewed her night-time sweats. In the absence of any disease, the doctor and Steph wonder if the problem relates to her psychotropic medications. Steph recounts her symptoms, and I suggest that she reduces and eventually stops taking venlafaxine. Curiously, Steph wants to stop taking her quetiapine medication, even though she thinks this is the drug benefiting her the most.

When I next see Steph I suggest to her we begin reducing her medication and take a fresh look at her experiences. Soon after our meeting, she sends me a written complaint, which includes a statement claiming that I'm known for being a careless and frequent prescriber: 'The word on the street is that anyone can get anything from you.' Hurt and angry, I never want to see her again.

Remarkably, some months later, when invited, she comes back to see me. In the interim, she's taken another overdose, is under the purview of the Mental Health Act and is now on five different medicines, including lithium, which, given its lethality, makes me nervous should she take another overdose. There is a statutory obligation under the Act for her to be seen by a psychiatrist, and Steph is in our area. I talk the matter over with the Director of Clinical Services at our local hospital. Supportive, she checks with the pharmacy to confirm that I am not a frequent prescriber and suggests that I invite Steph back with a support person in attendance. I ask Steph's case manager to be my support person! This time Steph cries, and this time I listen. I can see a real person who is genuinely hurting.

Steph is now striving to understand herself. Duncan, like me, had earlier tried to engage with Steph and had been hurt by her. A colleague once said to me that although we clinicians might think we're the ones who've been effective for the people we work with, the more likely scenario is that we're the ones who've been able to grow the seeds planted by our predecessors.

People come into or return to therapy by many different routes, including a complaint, as has been the case with Steph. Our ability to reconnect with her may have been due to our willingness to experience the same hurt that Steph herself has experienced throughout her life. This willingness to share the risk of exposure is revealed in the next story—Mara's.

'I've got plans'

Mara's background is one of physical and sexual abuse, but she partitioned this out of her life by reinventing herself. She changed her identity and country, and seemingly functioned well for several years. But when she returned to New Zealand and found out that the person on work placement with her had been convicted of physical abuse against children, she disintegrated. Distressed by continuous nightmares and flashbacks—'I can feel him all over my skin again!'—Mara went about killing herself. Attempts to engage her and to manage crises using brief respite care, hospital admissions and medications have been to no avail.

Nevertheless, Mara keeps turning up at our clinic to tell us what she's planning. 'I've done some research about how much I need to take, and I'm emptying my house.' We continue to offer our willingness to help, introducing her to the psychological approaches that we might take at her pace, inviting her to trial different medications at different dosages and to let us know what is helping. We write a letter to her outlining her distress and her understandable wish to die. However, we also point out to her that she must be in two minds about suicide because of her frequent visits to the clinic to tell us of her plans. We say we want to work with this healthy part of her. We hope the letter will be something she can hold on to, that it will give her hope.

At our next meeting, Mara tells us that she has tested and refined her suicide plan, and placed her animals in care. She reaffirms that while we might be willing to work with her, she is not. A further urgent home visit confirms that her house is now Spartan, devoid of much of her life. We talk there about how we might proceed. I have to be sure that there is a healthy part to Mara that is capable of being, as I tell her, 'a responsible and competent adult'. We offer and discuss with her our thoughts on the Mental Health Act, her ambivalence about treatment, and the prospect of compulsory hospital admission. We're concerned that the latter might contribute to further feelings of shame and powerlessness. Talk also turns to the fact that if Mara is admitted, she will still have to leave hospital in time and face her reality. We again invite her to work with us. Mara thanks us and declines our invitation.

We're anxious, given her clear intention to suicide, to leave her without committing her to hospital, but we also feel that this is the right decision. We have to trust our feeling that this is the right decision for this person at this time. We always have the capacity to use the law and admit someone to hospital. However, as we noted in one of the earlier stories, we can make things worse for the client in order to allay our own anxieties.

Fortunately, our instinct is reliable in Mara's case. She is now in therapy and, although struggling, is doing the work at a pace and with a medication regimen of her choosing. Encouraging Mara to shift from the passenger's to the driver's seat, helping her recognise that she is part of her problem, has enabled Mara to reconnect with the healthy part of herself that wants to live.

'I want to work on this'

A local physician phones through to my private practice to ask if I'll see a woman who's had anorexia nervosa for 30 years. Although I don't have a particular expertise or interest in anorexia, I want to help my colleague. However, I'm also aware of the clinical focus of and the financial reality of running a business as a private psychiatric consultant. Eventually, I say no.

Some months later, the same physician phones me to say that Paula wants to go into hospital in order to put on weight. The dietician and other health professionals are on board, and would I be prepared to consult? This time, I can say yes, because Paula's decision to go into hospital shows she is ready to take some responsibility for the work she, with our support, needs to do to get well.

I meet separately with Paula to clarify my role. The physicians will manage her feeding and the electrolyte and protein abnormalities of a person who weighs 28 kilogrammes (62 pounds) and has a body mass index (BMI) of 9.8. My interest will relate not to her weight but to getting to know her as a person.

We all meet with Paula to discuss what we might do. Although we're seated in a circle, Paula, interestingly, seems to be at the 'head' of it. Answers are sought to questions: When does Paula want to come into hospital? What are her goals? How can each of us contribute to her recovery? With Paula's concurrence, we agree that I will visit her regularly while she is in hospital, and thereafter we'll meet in my rooms.

All goes well. Everyone works together. Paula puts on weight and continues to see me until I leave the area. Although Paula does not meet criteria for BPD, there are traits of it in her story. That story, moreover, is so compelling and illustrative of our approach to working with people with this disorder, that I ask her if I can write about her. She agrees.

Paula and I have since often talked about what made the difference in terms of her recovery and were content to put it down to the alignment of the planets. But it was, of course, Paula's own realisation that something had to change. Once she had decided this, progress was relatively straightforward. All we had to do was to be patient and wait for her to accept her contribution to recovery.

'There's part of me that wants to change'

Rachel's behaviour is making a good number of people very nervous. She's attempted suicide many times, and her attempts to hang herself have been very determined. Twice, though, she has been found when she expected to be alone. Rachel uses suicide, thinking about suicide and self-harm as a way of escaping emotion she finds intolerable. What is striking is the degree to which she obsesses about the means of killing herself.

Rachel, at 21 years of age, carries with her a diagnosis of obsessive compulsive disorder. She speaks of the fixated nature of her thoughts of escape and describes her life as being one that is in constant pursuit of the means of her death. In our assessment session, she admits spending time considering the accessibility of my computer cables as a means of hanging herself. When I ask her what her life would be like without these constant thoughts, she admits to anxiety. I assume she is referring to the withdrawal of her much coveted means of escape, but Rachel asserts she simply cannot imagine what life will be like if she were able to think 'normally'; it's been that long since she has not thought about killing herself.

But Rachel's commitment to death is not total. I am sure clinicians' stories of successful engagement with acutely suicidal patients share common themes. How tempting it is to attribute the reasons for this engagement to one's own magnetic personality, I think wryly. Although at times over-stated, such engagement may indeed be an important factor. Despite the seemingly intractable nature of Rachel's difficulties, we are now gaining clarity on some of the vital ingredients that have led to her contemplating change.

First of all, she believes that medication, although helpful, is not the answer, and that 'sorting things out' is going to require therapy. Critically, she has not retreated into an unhelpful fusion of self and illness; rather, she sees her own role in maintaining her difficulties. Secondly, she has read about BPD and feels this diagnosis fits much better with her experiences than her current diagnoses of depression and obsessive compulsive disorder. We agree.

'I can get better'

Mila has long suspected she was abused as a child by her father. She has always been terrified of him. One of her earliest memories is of her mother calling her a slut when she was four years old after she played 'doctors and nurses' with another boy at playgroup. When Mila was six years old, her uncle started to isolate and sexually abuse her over a number of years. At the age of seven, she was subjected to a brutal anal and oral rape, the memories of which have continued unbidden in both sleep and wakefulness for decades since. When Mila reached puberty, her uncle expressed disgust about her changing physical appearance and rejected her.

One evening, as Mila, age 12, walked home from an after-school activity in the dark to gain a few precious minutes away from her parents, she was raped at knife-point. She felt so ashamed of herself she was unable to tell anyone. Three months later, she realised she was pregnant. She decided that she couldn't approach her doctor about her pregnancy and the reasons for it because the doctor, given Mila's age, would be compelled by law to disclose her pregnancy to her family. She was also well aware that her father, known for his violence, forbade any emotional response in others, seeing it as weakness. For Mila, death was the infinitely preferable option.

Required to attend a radical religious group with her family, terrified that people would be able to see what she had done and convinced that she was guilty of the sins being described in the sermons, she nevertheless approached a minister. He told her that her pregnancy was God's will. Mila eventually decided to have an abortion without being detected by anyone. She had, after all, become expert at hiding the impact of the abuse she'd been receiving for so long.

These events resulted in more unwanted, traumatic memories and the conclusion that all the bad things she had been taught about herself were true. Several years later, a girl at the same church sect watched while her boyfriend raped Mila. Then, as a young adult, Mila was used sexually by older men. These episodes were filmed and distributed to other men. In return, Mila received 'love' and financial support.

Given these experiences, I'm very surprised that Mila is able to describe these exact experiences in a single assessment. Her complexity and pathology are extraordinary, but she gives no indication of wanting to shock or elicit care and protection. She is clearly scared when describing these events, scared about imparting this information, but she rationalises that there is no purpose in not giving the fullest account of her life. More surprising still is that Mila is actually pleasant. She spends time discussing her enjoyment of the non-fiction she seems to absorb avidly (fiction she avoids because it's 'too full of cues'). When she leaves, she sincerely thanks me and warmly returns my firm handshake.

It seems inconceivable that someone can experience this level of trauma and abuse, have her trust in others so grossly violated, but allow, so bravely, a connection with a stranger—yet another therapist, and a man at that! Most striking is the clarity with which she describes the terrible things that have happened to her and, by virtue of post-traumatic stress disorder, continue to happen. Yet, she can, and this ability has remained evident throughout her ongoing treatment.

FURTHER COMMENTARY AND REFLECTIONS

Here, then, are representatives from three groups of people who present to our services. All of them have a diagnosis of BPD or exhibit traits of it. All are obviously distressed when they come to us, with their lives and those of their families profoundly affected by their interpersonal difficulties, affective storms and repeated attempts at self-harm. However, the groups differ from one another in terms of their readiness to make use of the help our team offer. The first group—Eva, Pat, Tom, Ness, and Jess—are not yet ready and therefore able to use that help, the second group (Steph and Mara) are midway to doing so, and the third (Paula, Rachel and Mila) have not only accepted our offer but also recognised that their health depends on them accepting responsibility for their recovery.

The first group are frightened and keep help at bay by being angry and contemptuous, by being silent or by simply not attending appointments. The second group are also frightened and tentative. However, with careful support, available over time, with they and us being honest in our reflections, sharing the risks of exposure and clarifying whose problem it actually is, are beginning to dip their toes into the water. The third group have immersed themselves in that water. Their courage has led to committed engagement with therapy, such that they begin to experience the positive difference that this commitment can bring to their lives.

The idea that if therapy is to benefit people, they need to see that they have a problem, are part of that problem and must be open to considering the nature of the problem is a well-developed one in mental health. Rachel's story in particular illustrates this point. The impetus for change ultimately came from within Rachel. She reached the conclusion herself that she needed to work with us to achieve success.

It would've been easy for us simply to talk to Rachel about this need to own and engage in her therapy without securing her buy-in to that idea. If we'd done this, we'd likely have fallen into a stalling therapeutic relationship, with Rachel sitting apart from any successful work she could potentially engage in. At one time in my practice, this was a scenario all too familiar to me. However, in time I came to see that because of people's different readiness to take ownership of their difficulties and to actively participate in therapy, we needed to *slow down*, to give them time to work towards that readiness.

I became interested in working with people with BPD as a psychiatric registrar. At the time, there was a requirement that admissions to hospital be discussed with and sanctioned by the consultant psychiatrist. I observed that despite the same people arriving time and again at the hospital, their management was determined not by what was happening in their lives, but by which consultant was on call at the time. Bruce tended to admit; Jeremy seldom did so. Yet nothing seemed to change for these people; well, certainly not for the better. I became intrigued. How could we better help this group of people?

Shortly after these experiences, I moved to Australia, where I found myself working with a group of five women who'd each spent an average of 316 days in hospital and between them had accumulated 2,400 hours of the special (one-to-one) nursing deemed necessary to prevent harm. Despite this approach, 76 incidents requiring transfer to the general hospital occurred. Typically, two of the women created a distraction at meal or medication times while the other three set fire to or tried to hang themselves. They also extracted razor blades they'd hidden in their vaginas just before returning from leave, and used them to slice their necks.

I was beginning to learn an important lesson. It seemed that whatever we tried to do made matters worse. We'd become frightened to do anything but commit these women to a mental hospital and provide special nursing. If we didn't, we reasoned, they'd kill themselves. But then we began to read of work being carried out in other health services and realised that it might be possible to care in a different way. Within a medico-legally supportive environment,[2] we began to work in a far less hurried and therefore less stressful way with people in the community using our service.

Duncan became interested in working with people with BPD by quite a different route. In 2008, while working in a mental health facility elsewhere in New Zealand, his team leader asked him to attend training in DBT. During this training, he became aware of the value of this therapy for people presenting with the characteristics of BPD. He has used it to good effect with such people since.

On my return to New Zealand via a period in the UK, various circumstances, not least of which has been my work with Duncan and the rest of our current team, allowed me to reflect on and refine with these colleagues the less-hurried practice I had first used over 20 years previously. [2] Although I hadn't appreciated it then, that time was the beginning of a quiet comfortableness brought about by not feeling hurried or acting hurriedly—of being able to wait, observe and reflect before formulating diagnoses and treatments for and *with* our patients. As we discuss later in the book, diagnosing BPD is often difficult. It is a disorder that, as the next chapter shows, can be mistaken for or conflated with other mental health illnesses and so lead to inappropriate or ineffective medication regimes and therapies. Taking time to look beyond an individual's 'alarming and bewildering' behaviour (as one of my former professors put it) gave us the confidence to work with people in ways that we have found increasingly effective.

---

[2] Common practice, often required under mental health legislation, is to hospitalise people at risk of harming themselves. Our observation that this process generally led to no useful change for people with borderline personality disorder made us consider the need for a different approach and of not hospitalising this group. But to do this, we needed to ensure that we and the hospital had worked through the necessary legal issues, such that we could proceed with our approach in a way that ensured, to the greatest extent possible, the safety of both patient and practitioner.

This work relies on people feeling sufficiently safe to tell and begin exploring their stories from a therapeutic standpoint. Safety relies on trust and shared understanding between person, practitioner and other members of the mental health team. Honesty needs to be there as well. None of these conditions will be in place immediately; they, too, must develop over time. While it might be easy for clinicians to form a fast diagnosis and treatment plan, we strongly consider from our combined experience that such an approach rarely offers long-term health gains for the person. And that's something the person needs to come to understand as well. Time, furthermore, is needed for people to reach the point where they can commit to the work they need to do, in collaboration with us, to help themselves heal.

We've found the taking time and slowing things down approach so valuable that it has become the platform on which we've developed the principles that today guide our practice in working with people with BPD. The amount of time needed to reach mutual understanding and effective therapeutic work can be considerable. Finally, both patient and practitioner may come to realise they have taken the work as far as the person can manage, and so mutually decide to leave it there. This is a matter we address later in this book.

Chapter 2

'With the Stroke of a Pen' … The Dilemma of Diagnosis

A hunch held lightly is a direction to be followed, not a decision to be defended—
Karl E Weick

In the last chapter, we described a group of people for whom the diagnosis of borderline personality disorder (BPD) was uncomplicated. Their stories, presentations and interactions unfolded for us with a familiarity and coherency. The stories we present in this chapter feature people who initially seemed to be presenting with other illnesses or whose diagnosis of this disorder remained 'hidden', meaning that it took time for the characteristic patterns and hallmarks of BPD to declare themselves and so be recognised as such by us.

Schizophrenia

'I'm fine'

Erica has stopped her injectable medication. She tells me and the members of my team meeting with her that she's fine. The side effects have disappeared, as have her voices, ever commenting about her, following her, wanting to kill her. She reminds us whenever she becomes upset during the session of her family's strong history of schizophrenia. 'I'm suicidal,' she says, but she expresses the words nonchalantly, all the while watching us for our reactions. She dismisses our concerns when she describes her attempts at hanging herself. Later in the session, she confides that she can always touch the floor with her toes when she starts to choke.

Erica's childhood included abuse and exploitation. The family were itinerant, school was intermittent and Erica soon became homeless before working the streets. 'He knows I've got a mental illness,' she explains in relation to her current relationship, although quite what she is intending to explain is unclear. We try to explore the relationship with her, which is obviously abusive, but she doesn't want to know, doesn't want to talk about it. All we get is that she, Erica, doesn't want to leave him; she wants medication. 'I don't want to think about it,' she says of her relationship.

Some months later, Erica returns, agitated and hallucinatory. Any taint of medication has long since disappeared, and I wonder if she might be relapsing into schizophrenia; the time frame is consistent, as is the family history. It would've been easy at this point for me to slip into the old familiar two-step approach of threat followed by hospitalisation. But there are other features of how she is presenting that are niggling at me, and I decide to wait.

I return to the matter of her relationship, but all I get is a single sentence: 'I know I should leave him, but I love him.' It's all too frightening for her to explore, and she quickly leaves. Two weeks later, she reappears. The relationship is fine, but the following day she is frightened. She's been without medication for some time now, and I've become nervous that my interest in psychological understanding may have taken precedence over actively addressing illness. Erica still wants medication, and I agree to prescribe. First, though, I venture again onto the topic of her boyfriend, and this time she tells me they've split up. In fact, she's been parted from him for some time. She isn't interested, though, in exploring if there is a connection between her relationships faltering and then her seemingly losing her mind. I still don't know if she has schizophrenia.

'I've got a psychosis'

Chris is referred to me for a repeat prescription. 'What's this for?' I ask. 'They say I've got psychosis,' the clean-cut young man in front of me replies. He then tells me that Satan and God talk to him, that he was brought up in a strict religious family and that he's been tempted to try new things but is too frightened to do them because they're evil. Satan, he explains, is an archangel whom God banished from Heaven because he disobeyed God.

Chris has been admitted to a number of different psychiatric hospitals in Australia, and he says that since being on medication, he can no longer tell whether the voices really are those of Satan and God or whether they are his own thoughts. There is no family history of major mental illness, although there is considerable conflict amongst the people within the cult where he was raised. My team and I are aware of this group of people who live on the fringes of the desert in the state where Chris grew up.

I decide it's not unreasonable to continue prescribing his medication, at least initially, but I do say to him that there are some matters I'd like to consider further, and would he mind if I spoke to someone else, such as his family? He does mind but, curiously, agrees that I can retrieve his interstate files.

These record his accounts of his imaginary friend, his anxiety about his sexual interests and his notion that he's adopted—all symptoms similar to those of other patients on his ward. Perhaps he thinks he's like the others so that he can fit in. It's becoming clearer to me that Chris's difficulties can be understood without introducing a diagnosis of schizophrenia, an understanding that we could have confirmed for him had he not moved on to another town in another state yet again.

'Because I want to!'

Jade weighs 130 kilograms (286 pounds). She sits motionless as her children clamber over and around her. Her mouth is half open, a pool of saliva spilling over her lip. Jade is again being overwhelmed by voices instructing her to kill 'him'—voices that have been part of her life for years. 'He' is an alien, and she, Jade, is the person destined to kill him. God has chosen her for this task and given her special powers so she can carry it out. But she misidentifies 'him' as another man whom she'd seen fleetingly and who had red eyes. What's more, the radio has been broadcasting that she and her children all have tracking devices within their bodies, and that beings from the other world inserted them. She is immortal, and she wants to cut the devices out. Previous medication, including clozapine, has not prevented six hospital admissions in the preceding 12 months.

Jade's background includes childhood sexual abuse from ages 9 to 12 and a violent stepfather who threatened to kill her should she disclose the abuse. His similar threats to Jade's mother led to both mother and daughter fleeing from their home. Amongst Jade's physical health experiences and symptoms are a pneumothorax, hemiplegic migraines, pseudo seizures and gallstones. There is a family history of epilepsy and bulimia but not of psychotic illness. I admit her to hospital for the seventh time this calendar year.

Shortly after, I am taken aback when Jade's new inpatient psychiatrist says that Jade has complex post-traumatic stress disorder (PTSD). I respect my colleague and decide to take a little more time considering Jade's case. It's clear that Jade's inpatient admissions have become increasingly frequent. Also, although there have been periods on the ward where those observing her described her as mute and thought-blocking, there are times when those behaviours seem characteristic of a person with BPD. For example, Jade one time was found repeatedly banging her head on the seclusion room wall after having tried to strangle herself. 'Because I want to!' she screams. 'I want to hurt myself! I'm not taking any fucking medication!'

When she is out of hospital in the community, my team's experience with Jade is as I described earlier. She is inert, swollen, overwhelmed by all that is in front of her. As a team, we begin to think about the family unit and what all her admissions might be like for Jade and her husband as a couple. 'Fine,' they each maintain, without effort or strain. We decide to probe a little more—gently at first, expressing our surprise but also our sincere interest in the couple's response.

It takes some months for the cracks to finally emerge. It's apparent that Jade's husband has become increasingly frustrated by Jade's constant readmissions, her staying in bed when at home and her inability to contribute to a busy household. The house is chaotic with strewn toys, un-ironed washing and overturned furniture.

After her latest admission, Jade was not discharged home but to a respite house, a step-down facility where people can go in order to avert admission or, as in this case, enable an early discharge. When psychiatric nurse Ruth and I visit Jade there, we notice something different. Although Jade has continued to describe her abnormal experiences and her suicidal thoughts to us, she smiles and waves goodbye as we drive away.

Her demeanour is at odds with what she's now telling us about her husband. Apparently, before she went into hospital, they had a huge fight, her husband no longer sure if he wants to stay in the relationship. He told Jade that he couldn't keep doing it all and suggested that it might be better for the children to have a constant parent figure, rather than one who's so often in hospital. Our team begin to wonder if the couple's fight may have precipitated a flight into madness. For Jade, hospital would be a legitimate way of leaving behind all the difficulties she has as a wife and a mother. We know that we have to have a conversation about this with Jade—gently, but honestly and openly.

The next day, we receive an urgent call from the staff at respite. Jade's husband has visited, and Jade's mental state has deteriorated further. Ruth and I are nervous. We know that if I admit Jade yet again to hospital, nothing will change for her. We also know that if our decision is the wrong one, she might kill herself and leave her children motherless.

On entering the respite house, we find Jade as we've seen her in the community many times before—sitting, rocking vacantly, saying she wants to die. We sit down. We try to talk to her, to quietly discuss our thoughts. Her responses, though monosyllabic, do indicate that she is taking in something of what we're saying. We decide to try a grounding technique that Duncan taught us. We ask the staff if they have a tennis ball. They don't, but offer a soft, bright-yellow squidgy ball. 'Would this be work instead?' It would.

I turn to Jade, who's sitting on the sofa across from me. 'Jade, we notice how you blank out sometimes. When that happens, I'm going to throw this ball for you to catch. Okay?' Why is it that the opportunity to try something for the first time seems to occur when it's most critical that it works, I think. As I try to explain the idea behind the ball-throwing to Jade, she blanks out. I toss the ball to her, apprehensively … and she catches it! We all laugh with relief.

Having got her attention back, we ask her how long she wants to stay in respite. 'Forever!' she replies. Tentatively, we resume outlining our observations and thoughts, suggesting to her that they coalesce around her marriage and the stress of motherhood. Perhaps, we put to her, her difficulties are her way of shutting out or leaving behind what has become unbearable? When we leave, we agree that our conversation with Jade has gone relatively well after all. Importantly, we have been true to ourselves. We've held to our decision about how to progress with Jade.

That night Jade comes downstairs from her room and tells staff that she wants to run away. 'I've had enough. God's telling me to kill the aliens.' She says that when she's like this, she has to go to hospital, but this time she doesn't want to. Although the staff know of our plan, they are frightened when Jade puts a cord around her neck and pulls it tight, voices all the while commanding her to kill herself. I readmit her for the eighth time in the year.

The following day, her husband announces he's leaving the marriage. With our plan in mind, we quickly ring the inpatient team to ask that Jade be discharged to respite, rather than repeat a further long period in hospital. We know matters might escalate for the worse as a consequence of returning her to respite, but we also know that we need to support Jade as she manages what we believe is her real terror—losing her husband and children. In discussing our thinking with Jade, we also underline our own fears and, perhaps as a result of sharing our vulnerability and effort to manage our tension, Jade is able to manage hers. She moves back to the respite house.

Time passes. Although there are tense periods when Jade believes that she has to cut the transmitters out of her body or that she will hang herself, we carefully and increasingly develop confidence in our new way of understanding by reflecting back to Jade our hypotheses and by seeing that she actually copes with our ideas. We are now able to build on the little things we notice, such as Jade making the same comment that we had made when with her some days earlier: 'If nothing changes, nothing changes.' She recognises that her threats were a plea and that she was frightened not only of changing but as to whether she could. For the first time, she acknowledges that her marriage and mothering need to change. Our diagnosis with respect to Jade also changes.

BIPOLAR AFFECTIVE DISORDER[1]

'It's my bipolar that's doing it'

Deb, with a modest IQ and difficulties in planning, organising and being able to recall strategies, has recently moved from the institution in which she has long been living to a home in the community. Time is needed to see and engage with a person with intellectual difficulties, so fortunately I have the opportunity (not always available) of reviewing her files before her appointment with me.

I read that, since leaving the institution, Deb has been experiencing brief manic phases characterised by poor sleep, jumping up and down on her bed as a manifestation of increases in her sexual drive and reporting demons outside her window. Her more common depressive phases have been characterised by deliberate self-harm, including voices commanding her to swallow bleach, gas herself in an oven and set fire to herself. Her presentation is further complicated by her medical history: hypertension from age 18, asthma complicated by pneumonia, resulting in respiratory failure and intubation, grand mal seizures and hypothyroidism. Amidst her many notes, a single sentence stands out. It states that Deb has fallen into 'the sick role', that her moods change within the hour and that when she in a manic phase, she is childlike and helpless. I hadn't expected these comments, as the behaviour they point to is not one consistent with classic bipolar illness.

Since moving into the community, where she's living in rented accommodation several streets away from her family, Deb has been repeatedly hospitalised because of concerns that she'll burn herself. She's been presenting out of hours with what turn out to be simulated asthma attacks. I learn she's also been standing in the local shopping mall wailing, seemingly uncontrollably, which initially elicited compassionate concern from the passing shoppers. People, however, have tired of this behaviour and want 'something done', as do her family members, who continue to visit Deb in her home.

'Hello,' I say on meeting Deb, who is small, her hair blonde and bobbed. She lifts up her top to show me her abdomen, which has just received a second skin graft. 'What happened?' I ask, and she tells me in detail how getting upset with her family led to her harming herself (most often by burning).

Over the next three years, our team don't see a single episode of an underlying bipolar affective illness. There is still distress, and there are presentations in the context of family conflict, but no classical depressive or manic states. Instead, we develop a better understanding of her distress, and we share that understanding with her. We become increasingly confident that we're engaging with a person who has difficulties managing her

---

[1] Recently, variants of classical manic depressive insanity have been suggested, partly in the hope of making available to people medication that better fits the characteristics of their illnesses.[3–6] So, for example, people who may otherwise have been given a diagnosis of borderline personality disorder have been reconceptualised as having bipolar affective disorder, particularly Bipolar II.

moods when she feels unwanted or exploited, and who firmly believes that she cannot cope in any other way than those that brought her to her initial appointment with me.

We're not so confident as to remove all of her medication! However, we continue to maintain our approach, repeatedly teaching and rehearsing different techniques for managing her distress. Evidence that Deb, in turn, is responding comes in the form of less contact with us and a greater reliance on her own abilities.

'Mommy, look at me!'

Kelsey hasn't slept for six days, instead walking the streets throughout the night. She says she's been hallucinating (her words) and then adds (with much hilarity), 'My meds weren't working, so I chucked them out!' She's been on clozapine plus lithium plus sodium valproate plus quetiapine plus clonazepam. I quickly scan her previous discharge summaries and read that after she'd been discharged two admissions back, voices commanded her to go to the local chemist, where she brandished a knife and demanded morphine so that she could kill her mother. Instead of giving her a 10-year prison sentence, the court system required her to be readmitted to hospital and treated for what was assumed to be a relapse of manic bipolar affective disorder. Her night-walks and casting aside of her medication convinces me to admit her again.

Over the next 11 months, Kelsey becomes unwell on 13 separate occasions. I've always thought I was good at managing bipolar illnesses, and wonder if I'm missing something. As I think about Kelsey and her presentations, I recall noticing when I first met her that her mental state didn't seem right for mania. She'd flapped her arms up and down as she just sat and giggled, only to settle down when we talked, a pattern of behaviour that my peers had also observed commented on. I dismissed all of this at the time because of my alarm at her history.

Other clues suggest that whatever Kelsey is experiencing, it might not be a bipolar illness. One of the student nurses, noticing a woman in the waiting room, asks if this person is Kelsey. The woman's whole manner is childlike, the nurse says. Kelsey often brings us baking, made when she is sleepless, but it's always beautifully cooked and presented, in a pretty pink dish; unusual activity for someone with disinhibited disorganisation of mind. Kelsey also actively seeks appointments, at odds with the often irritated reluctance that can characterise outpatient mania. Finally, Kelsey is exquisitely sensitive to medication. Even with the cautious addition of a single half tablet of a SSRI[2] on alternate days for a difficult depressive relapse, Kelsey switches into what I think is mania. I realise I have fallen into the same pattern as my predecessors of responding pharmacologically to each mood state rather than with effort to explore and understand the reasons for and significance of these moods.

When I first met Kelsey, she briefly referred to a difficult upbringing. Having been distracted by her documented history, I did not pursue this potential line of enquiry. Had I, I might've been able to see her as a person earlier, rather than as an illness being presented to me. In time, I find her real story lies in her nursing notes. They're difficult to retrieve from archives and nearly illegible, but they provide straightforward accounts of her story.

What especially strikes me is Kelsey's first admission to hospital, done so that she could avoid the custodial sentence. According to the notes, Kelsey was experiencing reduced sleep

[2] Selective serotonin reuptake inhibitor, a class of compounds typically used as antidepressants.

and heightened moods; she was over-spending and laughing inappropriately—all behaviours consistent with mania. However, staff also state that she appeared to be lucid and coherent, her organisational skills and concentration surprisingly good and, when they observed her discreetly, they considered her mood to be normal.

I read on through her notes. During interviews, she talked loudly but settled within minutes, particularly when staff strove to understand her predicament, difficulties, dilemmas. This account I find especially interesting, as it suggests therapy possibilities. Various other comments of note include her cutting down her medication or refusing to take it, events which occur in the context of ward conflict. This is an important feature of her notes because self-harm in the context of interpersonal difficulties is a feature suggestive not of bipolar illness but of a BPD.

One nurse, presumably also intrigued by Kelsey's presentations, asked Kelsey to complete the Dissociative Experiences Scale Test, used to screen for dissociative identity disorder, previously known as multiple personality disorder. She scores highly. This information along with a single-page report tucked loosely into the back of her file also proves critical to me gaining a better understanding of Kelsey. The report states that, at age 19, Kelsey was working as a hospital clerk. During this time a consultation liaison team saw her because of her uncontrollable asthma. The team members found it extremely difficult to know if she was lying, but eventually concluded that she was probably manufacturing her symptoms and recommended a diagnosis of factitious disorder, a condition in which the person feigns illness or exaggerates symptoms of an illness. By now, I am becoming increasingly certain that Kelsey is not experiencing bipolar illness.

It is with this knowledge in mind that I again sit down with Kelsey, ready to talk at length with her. We agree that the past year has been difficult. I carefully suggest that this situation cannot continue and that in order for change to occur, something has to be done differently. Kelsey is receptive. On behalf of our team, I write a letter to her, which she eventually gifts back to us.

Dear Kelsey,

We've been thinking quite a lot about you and, like you, have been worried about the 13 episodes where your mood has either gone up or down over 11 months.

This year, we all want to do it differently because if we don't, nothing will change. You in particular wanted to be settled in order that you might feel stable and go back to work.

When we're thinking about changing, we turn to thinking about you as a person rather than you as an illness. You told us quite a bit about your early life. Your father left when you were young, and your mother was violent, often at you because you had been his favourite. Your brother was also abusive and hurt you. After your parents split up, you tried to visit your father, but were sent away to boarding school. On those occasions that you tried to stand up for yourself, you were further punished.

These events have shaped the person you are today and your view of the world—love has strings attached, people will leave you, you're not good enough, and if you try and stand up for yourself, you will be punished.

How does a little girl survive? What does she do with all those feelings? At times, you have just wanted to hide in bed for days, hoping that it will all go away. This has been called depression. You have taken overdoses, cut yourself and put yourself at risk

> by changing your own meds, deliberately making yourself sick. We wonder whether you might have done this because you felt unable to manage your moods in any other way and that the only way anyone would want to care for you is by you being unwell or by you pleasing others. Whilst we have all appreciated your cooking (perhaps me more than most!), you don't need to; we'll see you anyway.
>
> The other things that have happened over the past year were unintended consequences. You had nicely used this phrase to describe what happened recently. Although you felt better after your phone call to the Samaritans, you went to sleep and hadn't rung them back to confirm that their suggestions helped. As you appreciated, they had little choice but to ring the police. The Crisis Team saw you up in the police cells before you ended up in the respite house in the middle of the night. Similarly, I had seen your difficulties resulting from an illness and felt that medication was the safest option. I looked at what I was doing last year and realised how quick I was to prescribe and to agree to respite, my unintended consequence of not seeing you as a person.
>
> When we thought about all those ways of coping, a common theme seems to be how we have both doubted that you might be able to manage some of your moods yourself. The aim of therapy is to enable you to understand what is happening, what might be making your moods unsettled and for all of us to act in ways that are helpful and without unintended consequences! It will mean that we will all have to change. For us, to see that we may have been 'killing you with kindness' by always agreeing to medication changes or admissions means acknowledging that instead we need to support you in managing your feelings and thoughts. We will need to watch carefully though so we don't miss a bipolar relapse.
>
> What could go wrong? It's going to be difficult because what we are looking at has been years in the making. We need to be gentle and work on this over the year, and we then need to look back to see what has changed. There may be setbacks, because we don't know yet what's illness and what's just being upset. It might be that you become angry with everyone, including us, for all that has happened or not happened in your life. You have had to cope in the best way you have known. One of the unexpected ways that might unsettle you is that you actually improve. You may no longer feel special. This is a difficulty that many people have faced. It is, however, part of adulthood.
>
> We are hopeful. You have already done well since moving here. Although there were 13 relapses last year, there was only one that resulted in a hospital admission. That was when I was getting to know you and had felt so anxious that I too believed that the only safe option was hospitalization. The next two relapses were in respite, but as we developed confidence together, we have been able to manage in the community.
>
> You recognized your role in the misunderstanding with the Samaritans and, importantly, you were able to make the connection between your recent low mood and the anniversary of an assault.
>
> We are not sure that we understand everything at the moment but what we are sure of is that you are likeable and that, as a team, we want to have a go at making a difference. The changes in the way we work together this year are all orientated towards you being able to achieve your goal of greater stability and of returning to work. Let's do it!

We continue to work with Kelsey through the following year. On one occasion, she again presents in an unsettled state, interestingly while her usual community psychiatric nurse is away, and she again turns up at the clinic with a box of freshly baked biscuits in her hands.

I am aware of the extenuating circumstance of her nurse's absence, but am concerned that Kelsey's experiences are distressing her to such an extent that she wants to go back on clozapine, despite gaining nearly 50 kilograms (110 pounds) in weight the last time she was on it. She says she is frightened, has only been able to get two to three hours of sleep of night and that her hallucinations are unbearable. She wants to kill herself. I agree to try a new medication. The relief on her face is immediate.

The next day, I talk the situation over with the team, somewhat embarrassed that I have been unable to 'hold the line'—to resist giving Kelsey the 'security blanket' of medication. I feel that I've been an easy touch—that I've too readily acquiesced to her request, particularly given our reformulation of her therapy. The team are kind to me. The trainees present ask me where I think her images of blood and decapitated heads come from: 'Was she in an accident?' I again feel embarrassed, because I've never asked Kelsey about this. I realise I've been too frightened to experience what Kelsey tries to manage every day.

Later, Kelsey tells me that the blood glows at night. Her description suggests what she is experiencing is not a true hallucination, but this is likely to be of little consequence to Kelsey because it means that the medication we're using to lessen or eliminate hallucinations are very unlikely to be helping her. However, this time when Kelsey again tells me about the beheaded bodies she keeps seeing, I ask who they might be. She tells me that they're her mother and brother. Kelsey's effort to procure morphine from the chemist so she can kill her mother and then her immediate attempt to cut her own throat begins to make sense. Her ambivalent feelings toward her mother mean that she is unable to act on her threat. Instead, she expresses her ambivalence by harming herself.

Depression

'Would ECT help?'

A well-respected, experienced private psychiatrist refers Bronwyn to me for a second opinion. He's been seeing this 37-year-old woman for a number of years, and during this time there's been little change in her presentation. I am flattered—a warning sign perhaps. For some reason that I am unable to identify, I invite Janice, an astute nurse who is also interested in people with BPD, to attend my first meeting with Bronwyn.

We find Bronwyn—lying silently on a bed in the general medical unit of a private hospital. The staff are unfamiliar with and frightened of 'psychiatric patients'. Bronwyn's lack of colour, vitality and life are what we immediately notice about her. Her hair is dull, straight and short; her clothes utilitarian and tawny. Replies are short and without energy. She eventually sits up forlornly, seemingly waiting.

Bronwyn, we learn, has been depressed for a long time. Everything about her is 'slowed down', and she's unresponsive to both psychotherapy and multiple and adequate trials of medication. As such, electroconvulsive therapy (ECT) is a reasonable option, but her private psychiatrist is still unsure and has sought me out for a second opinion.

Janice doesn't think Bronwyn has a major depressive disorder. Her instinct is that Bronwyn has BPD. While Janice understands the argument for ECT, she doubts it will work. Nevertheless, we decide to trial ECT, and Janice's surmise is validated: the treatment doesn't work and Bronwyn returns to the care of her private psychiatrist. When I ask Janice why she thought ECT would be ineffective, she points out Bronwyn's lack of communicable sadness.

Some years later, Bronwyn's psychiatrist retires. By this time I am in private practice and Bronwyn is referred on to me. I don't recognise her at first, but as her story unfolds, I make the connection. Bronwyn intimates that she also made a connection with me when we first met but had been waiting for me to come back and see her again. As we begin and continue to work psychotherapeutically, I slowly come to understand her forlorn look and what she's been waiting for—her mother, who died some years earlier. By the time we end our therapy sessions, she's beginning to wear colour.

'It doesn't get down to the deep stuff'

Michelle's big eyes well with tears as she just keeps looking at me, imploringly—help me! She, like Bronwyn, is slow, in part because of her 121 kilograms (267 pounds) of weight, but also in her quietness. Her history reveals self-critical thoughts that are pseudo-hallucinatory in form. When on the ward in hospital, she has been rocking, muttering almost inaudibly to herself, 'Hurt! Die! Kill yourself! Michelle bad! Fat ugly bitch! You're a failure!' At times, she's needed to be restrained from grabbing the cutlery of other patients, intent on using it to self-harm. However, when she has visitors, she is bright, smiling, animated. It's her pretend face, she tells me later. Multiple admissions and multiple medications have been unhelpful.

Aware of this background, I am reluctant to re-hospitalise Michelle. Instead, I see her on a weekly basis, aware of the various possible diagnoses evident not only in her file notes but also in my mind. Are Michelle's difficulties predominantly related to her personality style, a conjecture for which there is considerable affirmative evidence, a depressive illness, for which there is also evidence, or a combination of both?

I become increasingly anxious about continuing to manage a person in the community who has slowed down so much that she's barely able to speak and who's increasingly reporting strong suicidal urges. The thought of explaining to the coroner why I did not admit this woman and offered her a trial of ECT also plays on my mind. If she didn't respond to ECT, I would still have the safety-net of having used the most effective biological antidepressant available. So I admit Michelle and find she does respond to a trial of ECT. However, I and the hospital team caring for her are unable to keep her well despite medication, and we progress to maintenance ECT. The hospital's psychologist, who is monitoring for cognitive side-effects, confirms that she is improving.

The picture begins to change again though, when the director of the ECT unit quietly raises some doubts about the diagnosis. He's noted that Michelle brightens and has an easy and companionable relationship with the ECT team before receiving each treatment. The pieces of the puzzle are coming together. When we look again at her old notes, we agree there is evidence for a biologically based depressive disorder, but when Michelle's in a depressive phase, she actually presents with features typical of BPD. Nevertheless, we decide to continue ECT, given its aforementioned effectiveness in treating biologically based depression.

This decision is subject to further scrutiny when Michelle's ECT anaesthetist tells us that her blood pressure and oxygen saturation levels drop when she is under anaesthesia:

'Does she really need ECT?' he asks. We request an urgent cardiology review to help us determine the extent of risk, but the anaesthetist's concerns generate a further review of Michelle's history, and I begin to have real doubts as to whether ECT *is* right for her.

The next development occurs when another team member and I visit Michelle at her home. By this time, Michelle is receiving outpatient ECT and is apparently doing well. We walk up her stairs and she meets us at the door. She seems bright enough, but despite having had ECT that morning, she suddenly breaks down in tears as she begins to talk about her family, her difficulties and self-loathing. 'I don't think ECT gets down to the really deep stuff,' she sobs.

Her comment once again makes me pause, slow down, and think. Is Michelle definitely getting benefit from ECT or have both of us just come to rely on it, with me uncritically so? There is also the matter of my own ego. I realise I may have been portentously reminding myself that I was previously a director of ECT in another service and therefore know what I'm talking about when it comes to ECT. I begin to realise that all of this may have influenced my diagnosis to one that aligns with illness responsive to ECT. Over time, ECT has become a security blanket for both of us. For Michelle, it has been her 'pick me up', as she later calls it. For me it has had the comfort of a valid treatment of Michelle's assumed depression.

Michelle and I talk some more, eventually coming to recognise what has happened and why. And with that realisation, we are able to have a different conversation. Together, we wonder if we could phase out ECT. But doing so will not initially be easy because we'll have to re-envision Michelle's illness and find another way forward. I don't like riding horses, and the prospect of moving away from the comfort of my earlier diagnosis and treatment conjures up for me a very disquieting image. I see horses standing in the middle of a strongly flowing river, with me having to transfer from one wet and slippery bare back to another. The horses' spindly legs and steel-capped hooves, scrabbling to find a foothold on an equally wet and slippery riverbed, add to my fear.

I share this image with Michelle, and as we talk about it, we create a space devoid of agendas. We now have the freedom and confidence to really begin exploring her life, her hurts and her ongoing worries, which are many. We're at last able to speak together about that which has been unspeakable for Michelle. It is this rather than ECT that begins to make an abiding, positive difference for her.

'We've all done things we regret'

Sally is a tall woman. Although her background history is sobering, I see her only briefly, during which time she responds well to a modest antidepressant regimen. I discharge her from the clinic.

A year later she returns, banging her head against the wall in the waiting room, continually rubbing away at the palm of her hand, telling everyone of her need to be purified. Remembering the details of her past, I take a risk and say to her, 'I'm wondering if you might feel dirty?'

'We've all done things in the past that we've regretted,' she replies.

Sally grew up in a strict religious household, where she experienced sexual abuse, being treated as a domestic servant (as was her mother), satisfying the needs of others before herself and never daring to speak out for fear of being subjected to further strong criticism. She believes her home at the time was haunted. She remained obedient, quiescent, until an adolescent rebellious phase led to her drinking heavily. She was also raped at this time, became pregnant and had an abortion, after which she returned to the church of her childhood and early teenage years.

Sally subsequently married a quiet, introverted man, also from her church and who frequently travelled abroad. Life continued uneventfully for many years until an unfortunate coalescence of multiple personal, family and financial stressors. Sally woke abruptly one night when she saw lights, heard music and began to wonder whether she had been chosen for a higher purpose, the details of which were unclear. What *was* clear to her, though, was that she was being watched: cameras had been recently attached to the repaired telegraph poles in her street, and a covert surveillance team was following her.

Over a period of months, we see Sally weekly. At times, we shift her diagnosis back and forth from a depressive illness ('Mum used to get like this') to that of a person whose personality structure appears to be the outcome of considerable provocation. This latter view is supported by her psychotherapeutic response to our work. Together with Sally, we learn that she has initially been too frightened to speak to us about her experiences, a fear that we reframe as one arising out of religious dogma-based criticism. The inconsistencies in her unusual presentation, such as banging her head against walls, only arose when she was able to begin exploring the influences of her early life on her present predicament.

In particular, our team observe that if Sally's current psychotic experiences are indeed psychotic, they are out of proportion to the depressive presentation in front of us and in front of her husband and children when we visit her at home. Her demeanour is understandable, however, given that she's still constantly scrutinised and monitored from a harsh, critical religious perspective.

Eventually, Sally is seen out of hours and admitted to hospital. She has a major depressive disorder with psychotic features and responds well to medication. The clarity of the dispassionate observer is timely. Finding the right therapy for her has been a 'just in time' situation, because by the time of her admission Sally is intent on suicide.

As Sally improves, we talk about her background together. She is relieved, as she at last has an explanation that for her feels true to what has been happening to her for so long. I'm relieved and humbled. Although I've been practising psychiatry for many years, I still got the initial diagnosis wrong, which could have made for an irretrievable error on my part. I am yet again reminded how easy it is to get lost down a particular track, bewitched by the coherency and plausibility of the immediate story instead of pausing and looking less hurriedly at the person's lifetime experiences, and whether and how these may be colouring his or her presentation.

Further Commentary and Reflections

A couple of years ago, I attended a meeting on bipolar illnesses, during which someone commented that up to two thirds of people with treatment-resistant depression may have an undiagnosed bipolar illness. The following year, I attended a meeting on personality disorder. This time, someone commented that up to two thirds of people with treatment-resistant depression may have an undiagnosed BPD. The similarity of the two remarks reminded me of a clinical aphorism that I picked up during my training. In general, with treatment, people with otherwise uncomplicated depressive illnesses get better within six weeks. If the person is not responding by the end of the six-week period, other matters need to be considered.

That aphorism, in turn, helped bring home to me the difficulty not only of making a diagnosis but also of making it objectively. For example, as some of the stories above illustrate, I've been caught out trying to separate depression from BPD. What finally enabled me to see my errors in these instances was slowing down, standing back, reviewing the different pieces of information gathered over time, incorporating the observations of others, and reflecting on all of this information carefully and critically. It's remarkable how we see only what we want to see or see only a particular part of a person, much like the five blind men attempting to describe an elephant while only able to report on that which is in front of them, such as the trunk, the leg, the abdomen.

We might assume, then, that reference to traditional science-based research methods will bring us the objectivity we seek. But although often an arbiter in the diagnostic process, science, too, is limited. The seemingly simple process of observation is itself deceptive, as is the case with optical illusions and as it was for Bertrand Russell's turkey.

On his first morning at the farm, the turkey observed that he received food at 9 a.m. and wondered if he would be fed similarly next day, and the day after that. However, being a cautious bird and not wanting to jump to conclusions, the turkey waited until he had collected a large number of observations, under a wide variety of circumstances, of when he was fed. Every day, wet or cold, he was fed at 9 a.m. He finally concluded from his observations that he would always be fed daily at 9 a.m. However, his conclusion no longer held up when Christmas morning arrived.

The point of course is that despite our best effort to be objective when endeavouring to come to a diagnosis, there will still be a strong element of subjectivity, as is evident in the stories of the people featuring in this chapter. Different psychiatrists see the same patient and yet arrive at different diagnoses, a situation which may also indicate ideological preferences. British philosopher and educator Stephen Toulmin, reflecting on diagnostic approaches in different psychiatric departments, found that some departments tended to be influenced by 'objective knowledge', which meant their focus was on discovering the cause of psychopathological behaviour. [7] Treatment generally involved 'doing things' to the afflicted individual and treating him or her as the traditional passive patient. Other departments actively explored with the person the confused intentions underpinning the psychopathological conduct. Their approach usually focused helping individuals take responsibility for themselves—of treating them as responsible and competent adults.

Although maintaining that both kinds of psychiatry have a legitimate place, Toulmin argued that lithium and listening are not alternative ways of dealing with the same problem. In choosing one type of treatment over another, the psychiatrist has already decided whether to treat the individual concerned as an object or as a person. The risk of being treated as object is particularly heighted for involuntary patients, not just in theoretical terms but also social and institutional.

The dilemma for the psychiatrist caught up in this dichotomy can be captured in this question: How 'far' and in what respects am I to deal with this particular afflicted individual as a person who has the right to lead their own life and how far am I to treat him or her as an 'object' who requires intervention? We consider that this question can also be stated in terms of power: How should I best exercise this psychiatric power of mine, and to whom am I answerable?

A carefully set-up and conducted inpatient setting can be instructive in terms of formulating diagnoses and subsequent appropriate therapies. Experienced staff can test hypotheses by unobtrusively observing patients and their interactions with others. Repeated angry outbursts and acts of deliberate self-harm (including suicide attempts) in reaction to interpersonal stress and reflecting extreme sensitivity to rejection are axiomatic of BPD. These behaviours can be especially prevalent at the point of discharge, or when the person is required or even elects to assume increased personal responsibility.

Staff also need to consider if their feelings about a person are a manifestation of countertransference,[3] and, if so, what information this might usefully provide in terms of diagnosis. The depression-based experiences of emptiness, of meaninglessness, of being alone, with a view of oneself as fundamentally evil or despicable, are also characteristic of BPD. Overspending needs to be differentiated from retail therapy; overfamiliarity needs to be differentiated from seeking intimacy when feeling alone, dejected or abandoned.

Although some practitioners are outraged if colleagues question their judgements and diagnoses, others welcome differences of opinion in order to avoid John Stuart Mill's 'deep slumber of a decided opinion'. [8, p.54] Mill also warned that to compel a different opinion to silence is to assume our own infallibility. Different ideas and robust discussion should be welcomed. If the other person's opinion is right, then what we gain is the opportunity to exchange error for truth. If that colleague is wrong, we all gain what is possibly an even greater benefit—'the clearer perception and livelier impression of truth, produced by its collision with error'. [8, p.24] In other words, receiving confirmation of our judgements enables us to feel securer about our decisions and the way forward for our patients.

Sometimes the person is unhappy with not receiving the diagnosis they habitually expect. For example, I'd felt quite pleased that I'd been able to unbundle Michelle's difficulties and remove the stigma of a diagnosis that had haunted both her and her family. She was not! But then she paused, before adding thoughtfully, 'Perhaps now I can start to look at those problems.' As such, she avoided the defensive use of diagnosis and was in a space where she could subsequently explore and confront painful realities.

Diagnosis is a dance: either party can accept or decline the invitation. Until we secure revolutionary 'fail-safe' understanding in psychiatry, uncertainty will continue. We can manage the associated discomfort by imposing structures and strictures on our practice rather than by accepting that science, therapists and patients alike are not perfect but fallible. Such acceptance allows us a more gentle, humane and realistic approach to the clinical dilemma.

Given that diagnostic certainty is not possible, maintain a curious stance. Keep asking yourself what others, including the patient, might be seeing that you are not yet able to see. Explicitly acknowledge that practitioners' responses reflect a variety of biases peculiar to each practitioner. When clinicians voice these biases and discuss them with their patients, they open themselves up to developing shared understandings with those persons of the genesis of their illnesses. We consider this respectful synchrony another manifestation of the unhurried gentleness that enables reliable diagnoses and effective therapy.

---

[3] Countertransference refers to the situation of the therapist developing thoughts and feelings about the patient that, if examined, may give the therapist clues as to what is happening for the patient and how he or she relates to others.

PART TWO: TAKING RISKS

Our lives only improve when we make changes and the first and most difficult risk we can take is to be honest with ourselves—Walter Anderson

Chapter 3

EMERGING PRINCIPLES

Treat people as if they were what they ought to be and you will help them become what they are capable of becoming—van Goethe

Two unrelated incidents, occurring some time ago, prompted our decision to write down the principles informing our practice. Deployment of each of these principles requires both clinician and person to engage in varying degrees of risk-taking or, to use, a more colloquial expression, to work outside their comfort zones.

The first incident occurred during a symposium in Canberra, Australia. My group was one of three invited to outline our approaches to working with people with borderline personality disorder (BPD), and we were third on the podium. The first two groups outlined the success they were having with their approaches, both different. Our approach was different again, but also suggested hope. During my part of our presentation, I offered an observation and a question: 'How is it that seemingly different approaches to treating illness yield similar promising results?'

The second incident involved a conversation that began when my phone rang: 'Would you take a call from a GP?'

'Sure, put them through,' I said.

'Hi, I'm wondering how to treat someone with a personality disorder.' He sounded young and spoke softly.

It wasn't the sincerity of this general practitioner's request that embarrassed me; rather, it was my inability, as our conversation progressed, to briefly and clearly summarise our ideas on treatment to someone interested and on the front line. As I sat after I'd put the phone down, I thought about what I'd said, or tried to say, and realised that our team needed to clarify our thinking about the ideas underpinning the way we worked with our patients with BPD. If we couldn't articulate our ideas to ourselves, how could we expect to explain them to others?

My questions since those incidents have gained greater cogency, given the number of acronym-based therapies that have arisen in recent years. We have ACT and CAT. Then there is CBT, DBT and MBT, and also ITP.[1] Each has its champions, each of whom expresses

[1] ACT = acceptance and commitment therapy; CAT = cognitive analytic theory; CBT = cognitive behavioural therapy; DPT = dialectical behaviour therapy; MBT = mentalization-based therapy; ITP = interpersonal therapy.

enthusiasm for the style with which they connect and feel most comfortable. But what if these practitioners aren't available, if they accept promotion or transfers, as is often the case in public practice, when an existing or new patient presents? There is every possibility that the practitioner coming in 'behind them' is either not conversant with the favoured approach, has one of his or her own or has very little idea of how to proceed on the basis of what has gone before.

Ongoing discussions with colleagues and team members prompted the realisation that the various approaches, including our own, are underpinned by one or more principles that any practitioner can reference, even if he or she has little knowledge of the lexicon-informed therapies. Our interest, therefore, came to lie in distilling a 'simplicity' for clinical practice by refocusing on these principles, all articulated in an older literature but perhaps forgotten or 'misplaced' through lack of explicit articulation over the ensuing years.

In this chapter, we present relatively brief accounts of our development and use of each of these principles, namely, exhibiting a humane understanding of the person, having the courage to say no to them as a therapeutic tool, and encouraging them to assume self-responsibility within the context of therapeutic work. We follow these descriptions with further commentary and reflection on the value of these principles in our work with people with BPD.

PRINCIPLE ONE: EXHIBIT A HUMANE UNDERSTANDING

Nothing Happens Until the Doctor Is Touched by the Patient

In 1999, a small group of us convened a two-day workshop titled 'Caring in a Different Way: An Organisational Approach to the Management of People with Borderline Personality Disorder'. [2] Some years later, having explored further the ideas we presented and discussed then, we published an article about what we had learned. [1]

As we explained in the article, we'd begun our exploration of 'doing things differently' by talking to women whose suicide attempts had resulted in their involuntary detention in hospital within six days of their initial admission to hospital. As we spoke with them about these attempts, we learned that self-harm usually had developed early in their lives and as a result of intolerable distress. Each of these women had been sexually abused at a mean age of 7.2 years of age, believed that she was fundamentally loathsome and that nobody would want to be with her. For these women, suicide had become the only option, and once they'd considered it, the means of bringing about their deaths consumed their thinking: 'It's like a drop-down menu,' was how one of them put it.

We also gained a renewed appreciation of the need for humane understanding of deliberate self-harm as we put together a model of care for people for whom deliberate self-harm is the 'calling card': 'Everyone wants to be liked, but because it's my fault, no-one will want me. But if I try to kill myself, at least someone has to see me.' Central to our model, therefore, was the need for staff to reconnect with their patients' humanity, such that both parties (staff and patients alike) understood that 'You don't have to harm yourself; we will see you anyway.'

Sometimes, we needed to reinforce this principle for a person in a way that might appear foolhardy to some. For example, over a lengthy period of time, I regularly met Caroline, one of my patients, on Thursday at noon, no matter what happened. Importantly, though, I impressed on her that I would not meet with her at other times. Therefore, when the hospital's emergency department rang to tell me that Caroline had again turned up, having harmed herself, I asked them to remind Caroline that I looked forward to seeing her at the usual time and would the department please discharge her home.

Another patient, Stuart, frequently filmed himself cutting himself and sent the clips electronically to a senior politician with the message that Stuart's death would be on the their hands. Having done that, Stuart would contact the police to tell them he was going into the city, where he'd jump off a building in full view of those who he felt were responsible for his homelessness and unemployment. No one ever helped him, he said. Mental health services were useless, and so he was going to die. His emails to the politician and to us were inflammatory, uncomplimentary and in capitals. He also sent us faxes, scrawled across with the same spillage of fury and frustration.

I was trying to be my tolerant best when Stuart's deliberate self-harm precipitated yet another dispatch of police, a crisis team and an ambulance. Our clinical director was summoned to the state minister of health's office. 'This has to stop,' she was told. Stuart's threats towards higher authorities had become intolerable. We'd been working with Stuart, but he remained on the periphery of his treatment. We were also trying to write this book, and yet there he was, every morning on the fax machine. 'Damn him!' I thought.

But when I cooled down, I reminded myself of our principle of humane understanding. I realised I had lost sight of Stuart, and knew that I had to take a deep breath and start again. And the need to start again was what I told Stuart when next we met. Curious, I asked him why he always rang services after he'd harmed himself. Stuart paused before quietly replying, 'I don't want to be one of those people that's found dead in their flat weeks later.' This simple and sad statement began his and my understanding of how Stuart had never felt significant—had never felt wanted by either his family or his school peers.

Over the next few months, Stuart continued telling his story. By the time his learning difficulties at school had been identified, it was too late for him, and he left school, still alone. His interests reflected his isolation. They involved solo pursuits and little contact with others. It wasn't until his twenties, however, that he decided that he'd act in a way that meant he'd never go unnoticed again. Our task was to help him see how this strategy, which ironically had enabled him to survive, had now outgrown its usefulness. [9,10]

Today, with the learning we gained from the women who helped us coalesce our thinking regarding Principle One and our experience of that principle in practice with people such as Caroline and Stuart, this is what I'd now say to the pleasant young GP who had found me at a loss all those years ago. 'I have to feel something for the person and their story. When I get lost or angry, I have to remind myself to find them again, to ask what's happened rather than why they've done what they did.' I'd also emphasise that I'd want to see the person regularly, something that is particularly important in terms of us both (patient and therapist) learning to hold on, to tolerate terror, until we can talk it through at our next appointment.

Principle Two: Say No

> The fable of the camel's nose
>
> The camel, it will be recalled, asked leave to put his nose inside the merchant's tent on account of the cold weather. This favour granted, he proceeded, by means of flattery, deprecation, ridicule and logic to insinuate himself gradually and totally inside the tent. There was no longer room for the merchant, who was then forced out into the cold, warmed only by the scorn of the camel for his foolishness ....
>
> The beginning psychotherapist finds himself [or herself] in the merchant's shoes when he grants permission to his anxious patient to telephone him when anxiety becomes unbearable. Soon, no part of his life is exempt from intrusion, while curiously enough, no improvement has occurred in the patient's symptoms. [11, pp.32–33]

As a medical student, I was asked to commit a family member. Having completed a psychiatric attachment at the time, I approached the director of my unit to ask if Dr X rather than Dr Y could see my relative. Dr Y lived in the same town as my relative. Dr X did not. The director, an older man, quietly spoken and thoughtful, gave me a warm smile before replying, 'No.' His refusal was the point at which I began thinking about the appropriateness and value of saying no within a mental health context. The memory of that encounter with the director has also reassured many times over when I've elected to say no. One such time involved Carla.

Carla had recently moved to our area. Statutory authorities had removed all of her children from her care, and she'd become increasingly suicidal. Although we didn't know Carla and her circumstances, her request for respite care was reasonable, considering what she told us of her situation. But then she asked the team to take care of her dog. There was something about the way she asked this that made us hesitate; the request was not a reasonable one. Our subsequent decision—we said no—was a moment that defined and so continued to shape our subsequent relationship with her. 'The other team does!' Carla blurted out. But we held the line, and Carla managed herself.

One Friday afternoon some time later, Carla trod the familiar path to our mental health service. She'd again been evicted from her accommodation, and she wanted our help to find a new place to live. Sitting in front of me, she insisted on her inability to find something for herself: it was up to me, to our team, to help! I sat quietly for a moment or two after I'd said to her that I genuinely didn't know what to do to help. I'm such an impractical person for a psychiatrist, I thought to myself. But then I thought some more. Was this another reasonable question on Carla's part? If it wasn't, then the answer had to be no. I did ask her, though, how she'd previously found places and calmly reassured her that if she'd done this before, she could do it again. Once more we held the line, and once more Carla managed. She not only found a place to stay but also a job.

When I saw Carla again and pointed out what she had been able to do, she gleamed. Immediately after our meeting, I wrote the following letter to her.

> Dear Carla,
>
> Sorry to have missed you this morning and thank you for ringing up to advise that you were both well and didn't need to come along to your appointment today.

> This is just a wee note to let you know how proud we are of your achievement. As we discussed at our last meeting, you have been able to do this yourself. You found a job, you have been able to manage your home circumstances by keeping yourself in a safer place and you have been able to get on with your life.

For Ann, the principle of saying no was made apparent to her in a way quite different from that for Carla. I first met Ann as an inpatient of some months' duration. As I introduced myself, she provocatively demanded discharge. 'I'm fine,' she emphasised. 'I'll be safe. I'm not suicidal anymore.' I said I'd like to get to know her a little better before making a decision, and after some further remonstrance on her part, we agreed to meet weekly for an hour on the ward.

Here, the story of being misunderstood and rejected by one's family of origin, familiar to me because of its occurrence in the lives of so many people, but of singular and heart-breaking importance to each, became apparent. Ann's attempts at trying to survive while still in her parents' home involved inflammatory interactions that precipitated her, as a means of escape, into an early marriage.

I experienced her rage during one of our early sessions, when she screamed at me, abruptly left the room and, still angry, threw a chair across the hospital lounge. However, she threw it in such a way that none of the people in the room at the time was hurt. I tucked this fact away in my mind, as it meant Ann could still show care for others and therefore some control over how she manifested her anger. Somewhat later, Ann returned to my room, where she stood limply in the doorway. 'You didn't get angry with me,' she said, bewilderment colouring her voice. What's more, I'd neither medicated nor secluded her for being angry, and this also astonished her, but in a good way. From this time on, Ann and I really began to engage, and in time to seriously consider her discharge, even though some members of our team were sceptical about the wisdom of this. What happened next was, at least for the points being made in this chapter, the relevant part.

Ann's husband, who had never visited Ann in the hospital, suddenly wanted access to his wife's file. He demanded to see me despite Ann being clear that she didn't want him to do so. Not unexpectedly, the nature of their relationship had changed as a result of the work our team and Ann had done together. Ann had become more confident and assertive in regard to her husband. (Changes in the dynamics of a person's relationships with family and friends tend to be a side-effect of psychotherapy.) An articulate man, Ann's husband began wielding the considerable power and influence that people with this characteristic often display, channelling his increasingly angry demands through the various institutional processes available. Despite an understandable wish by complaints, quality-assurance and freedom-of-information agencies to appease, the non-clinical members of our team remained resolute in their desire to respect Ann's wishes. Without disclosing personal information, we had emphasised to them the importance of modelling the fact that it is possible to stand up to threats and pressure by simply saying no.

Although Tracy, each time she visited us, initially walked quietly into the clinic, she'd soon turn abruptly, aggressively, take a breath and shout at all within hearing, 'Why don't you listen!' Despite her tiny frame, everyone would jump. Her behaviour was certainly not conducive to the calm atmosphere we wanted for our patients and team.

The first time Tracy came in, wheeled around and yelled, we were caught off balance and hastily ushered her into a side room. Our reception staff, superb, experienced and understanding, did their best to contain Tracy's actions, but soon they, along with the people in the waiting room, wanted all of us to work together to find a way to modify her behaviour. We discussed Tracy at our weekly team meeting and began to explore what might be happening for her and for us. We initially decided we'd refrain from reinforcing her 'entrances' by not seeing her immediately, and then agreed that we didn't want to escalate the situation by taking this action.

Duncan was particularly helpful in this regard, and guided us towards a different response—one that would be appropriate within the context of a busy waiting room. The response had to be concise, Duncan explained, so that we could easily remember it despite the startle and anxiety that comes with being ambushed: 'Tracy, please stop shouting and talk to us quietly.' This simple statement, spoken with certainty, surprised us in its effectiveness. Tracy immediately quietened, and this time, of her own volition and in front of the others in the waiting room, she went to the side room. Our follow-up statement was similarly clear: we said to her that we understood she was hurting but that the only way we knew how to help her was for her to sit down regularly with us so that we could talk together.

These four encounters illustrate the effectiveness of our second principle—that of (respectfully) saying no. [11–16] This principle is not a new one. Its antecedents, derived from clinical experience, lie well back in the literature on managing manipulative and disruptive behaviour. A careful summary of its credentials can be found in an excellent paper written over 50 years ago:

> If inappropriate or untoward demands are not met the patient will not become sicker. The patient may complain bitterly, may make things more unpleasant, for those nearby, or may report increases in symptoms, but beyond this initial flurry, no clinical evidence of worsening of his condition is seen. The fact that this is found repeatedly to be true is of the utmost importance to the decision to set limits. [11, p.33]

Unexpectedly, it is the addiction and renal literatures that best confirm the efficacy of the 'no' principle. One important such study featured a methadone programme. Staff noted that although the programme was generally successful, some patients were jeopardising the programme's credibility because of their ongoing use of illicit drugs. The researchers randomly assigned 69 patients on the programme to either a 'structured' treatment group or a control treatment group.

Over the next two months, all 69 patients were required to submit urine samples, which were tested for use of illicit drugs. At the end of this period, both groups received letters asking them to meet with their counsellors. However, there were two forms of the letter. The one to the control group said that illicit drug use had been detected in urine samples and expressed general concern about this matter. The patients' methadone treatment continued as before. The letter to the treatment group expressed the same concern but also included a warning. Any members of the group who delivered urine samples containing evidence of illicit drugs at any time during the next four months would be placed on irrevocable methadone withdrawal and forced to leave the programme.

Twelve months on, the structured treatment group had achieved significantly more months free of illicit drugs than the control treatment group. In addition, fewer of the structured than the control patients had left the methadone programme during that time. [15] As one commentator on this study stated, 'placing even modest expectations on patients and backing these up with contingencies had a beneficial effect on treatment outcome.' [17, p.154]

The reaction of patients discharged from methadone treatment has been likened to infants' reactions on being separated from their mothers (as described by John Bowlby and Mary Ainsworth's in their 'attachment' studies). [18,19] It has also been likened to the reactions (observed and documented by Elisabeth Kübler-Ross) of people facing their own death or experiencing the death of a loved one. [20] For the methadone patients, there is initial disbelief, followed by anger, panic and distressed family contact, until they accept the situation, begin to mobilise their resources, and continue the task of recovery, which may include joining a support group.

Another valuable paper within the context of our present discussion documents the case of Brenda Payton, who took issue with her nephrologist after he said he would no longer dialyse her. [16] Payton asked the California State Court to compel him to do so. Eventually, Payton and her physician agreed on the terms of a court order that required her to comply with certain conditions, and dialysis resumed. After nearly a year, the nephrologist again notified Payton that he would no longer dialyse her, and again Payton filed suit against him. This time, she also sued two local hospitals that had refused to treat her in their dialysis clinics. Payton contended that her nephrologist was trying to abandon her and that the two hospitals were violating their obligation to provide emergency care.

The court, however, found that Payton had violated every condition of the order and had caused her nephrologist and other members of his team considerable ongoing stress. She had continued to use barbiturates, failed to restrict her diet, frequently appeared for treatment late or at unscheduled times in a drugged or intoxicated state, upset other patients and swore at staff members. Over an 11-month period, she was hospitalised on an emergency basis 13 times. The court held that neither Payton's nephrologist nor the hospitals were required to treat her. It ruled that the nephrologist had not abandoned Payton because he had given her sufficient notice of his desire to end their relationship and ample time to find another treating physician.

The court also observed that a chronic need for regular medical treatment did not constitute a need for emergency care at the two hospitals under consideration, even if the treatment required was life-sustaining. However, the court maintained that Payton would be entitled to dialysis in acute emergency situations, but that it could not order the hospitals to provide dialysis on a continuing basis.

Four years later, the California Court of Appeal affirmed the state court's decision. However, subsequent to this affirmation, the dialysis clinics in Payton's local area arranged to share the responsibility for her dialysis so that her treatment could be provided without any one clinic suffering an undue burden.

This case shows that saying no is not necessarily easy—that it's often frightening for patient and practitioner alike. It is, however, entirely necessary if someone is to begin contemplating their role in and responsbility for changing their lives.

In exploring the therapeutic use of no in general and with respect to BPD, we found little of relevance in the literature, but what we did find was positive. In one account of normal child development, we were reminded that when young children are being weaned from breast-feeding they're also being introduced to many new and potentially exciting foods. Young teenagers, one moment excited the next apprehensive about a party, protest when their parents refuse to let them go, but thank them later in life for keeping them from harm. The parents, believing in their decision, care sufficiently to say no. Opportunities presented within a secure environment make it safe to leave, in time, that which is familiar. Feeling secure is an important precursor for separation (individuation) and responsibility. [13]

Given the lack of literature, we can usefully consider limit setting in the psychopathological literature as a proxy for the concept of 'no'. Articles in the *Journal of Infant, Child and Adolescent Psychiatry*, for example, highlight the debate between a boundaried and a liberal position on limit setting. [21–23]

The liberal approach, in this case with regard to the child, claims that therapy should not be about engaging in a battle for control. Rather, it should allow youngsters to experience themselves acting out and breaking rules so that they become aware of and learn to use their own internal brakes. External attempts to provide controls for them will only undermine their own sense of uncertainty. [22] The liberal approach within the context of therapy lets children join with their therapist to face their difficulties, such that they are no longer perceived as 'monster' but as children who are confused, scared and extremely anxious. The boundaried approach maintains that containment brings relief to the desperate child. Parents and services who fail to provide boundaries by retreating, rewarding or retaliating overlook the importance of this developmental task.

Diana Ehrensaft has attempted to reconcile the two positions by exploring the social context. [23] She argues that democracy has replaced patriarchy, with parents wanting to be friends rather than authority figures. The adage of 'spare the rod, spoil the child' has given way to parenting by guilt, which, Ehrensaft says, leads to poor limit setting. Without clear boundaries, children and adolescents can enter adulthood believing they are invincible and that ordinary rules do not apply to them. The critical task for the therapist is to hold firm at the 'contact boundary'—to tolerate challenging behaviour. But with limits now in place, the person becomes angry, and buried feelings become frighteningly reawakened. The clinician is left with the task of trying to solve the problems of domestic violence, a person's delinquency or mounting debt.

> It is often not easy to set limits, especially when children are at risk, and statutory responsibilities can compel a clinician into collusion with the manipulative client. There are bound to be occasions when this seems to be unavoidable, but it needs to be borne in mind that it can only perpetuate the clinical problem of dealing with anxiety in this fashion. The relevant question is to ask whether we are preparing the person in problem solving or are we moving, however imperceptibly, towards collusion and avoidance. [24, p.26]

Like the 'confused, scary and terribly anxious child', the person with BPD is also frightened. The term 'attention seeking' does nothing to neutralise the terror, fear and aloneness of the person in crisis, where reasoning has no effect and freedom of action offers only panic. Although repetitive thoughts and actions, including suicide, may represent a form of active mastery for the person, it produces anxiety for those around them. For the person with BPD who cannot readily communicate their distress through words, this small measure of control is satisfying in a life characterized by limited, if any, expectations. [25–28]

In line with observations evident in the child literature, the therapist's feelings about people with BPD for whom wanting to die is a way of life can be less than therapeutic. Faced with the person who's always threatening to cut off their nose 'to spite your face' and in a world where you have to care more about them than they do about themselves, [25, p.100] therapists who know themselves 'deeply will be aware at times that [they] would like to make the patient suffer. [They] will feel anger and, beyond anger, sadistic impulses to retaliate.' [26, p.161] Ability to accommodate these feelings is important.

> These turbulent patients often leave treatment in very abrupt and unprocessed moments. It is suddenly all over and that is that ... We cannot always prevent this. Rather than seeing this as a complete failure ....struggling with these is critical to our ability to help such patients because these are the exact issues that the patients cannot bear in their lives, and if we cannot bear them, then the patient has no hope of ever surviving them. [29, p.23]

According to George Murphy and Samuel Guze, limit setting enables the establishment of a secure base from which the person can experience a wide range of new feelings. [11] The effectiveness of limit setting, however, relies on a genuine understanding of how difficult it is to put into practice. The fable of the camel's nose which began this section of the chapter is illustrative.

A consistent message across the limit-setting literature is that acting out in its various forms is the defence most difficult to penetrate; if not addressed, it can subvert the psychotherapeutic process. [11,12,30,31] We agree with the former CEO of Apple Incorporated Steve Jobs, who said, 'It's only by saying 'no' that you can concentrate on the things that are really important.' If we don't attend to unaddressed issues, we're not doing do our job. The consideration then becomes one of not whether to, but how and when: 'If very serious forms of acting out are not controlled, a fiasco may result in which therapy turns into just another avenue for the patient's habitual pathology.' [31, p.433]

So, my second set of comments for the GP would revolve around telling him that our team now recognizes that saying no not only to our patients' acting out through threat and deliberate self-harm but also to our *own* acting out in terms of inappropriate diagnoses and prescribing has freed us up to work on what is most relevant. If the GP then asked me if the approach works, I'd tell him that our team have found the therapeutic use of 'no', when thoughtfully and respectfully applied, enables both parties in the therapeutic relationship to experience a renewed enthusiasm that is reflected in better attendance, morale and outcome.

PRINCIPLE 3: 'MY PD'S BACK!' - ENCOURAGE RESPONSIBILITY FOR SELF

If you want to see what children can do, you must stop giving them things—
Norman Douglas

I had an amused respect for Sue's feistiness, her rebellious streak, and I think she felt the same about mine. It was not difficult for us to decide to work together so that Sue could get out of hospital and on with her life. With this resolve, came excitement. And then came the family's reaction, which neither of us had expected. I received a long letter from one of her children, written with a view to it being produced in court. Its message to me was clear: 'If you let my mother go and she kills herself, I will hold you, Dr Little, personally responsible!'

In the middle of the night, the local hospital phoned me. Fifteen-year-old Amanda has threatened to leave. She can't be persuaded otherwise, and could I come in and detain her under the Mental Health Act? Amanda's constant self-harm had led the supervisor of the shelter for homeless girls where Amanda had been staying to bring her to the hospital, which had decided to admit her. I hadn't met Amanda before, so when I arrived at the hospital, she and I sat and talked for an hour or so. She didn't like the nursing staff or their rules or regulations: 'What's the point in staying? They don't do anything.'

I invited Amanda to swap chairs: 'You're the psychiatrist, and I'm you. What would you do next?' Amanda took up the challenge, and we batted familiar arguments back and forth until together we confirmed her capacity to consider, weigh and communicate her decision about what to do next. She'd lived on the street before and knew that she would be safe. I discharged her from hospital. The supervisor was furious.

A colleague and I stood in the corridor talking about Zita, who has a rare neurological disorder. Although subtle, neurocognitive changes that were likely to intensify over time had been documented. 'She can't make decisions for herself,' my colleague told me. As a nurse who had been practising for 20 years, he'd seen many things, but changed little in his approach to patients. Sensing something—perhaps I had stiffened slightly—he corrected himself: 'She can't *reliably* make decisions. She has to be under the Act, and for her own safety, she has to be in seclusion.'

I'd been asked to see Zita in order to give a second opinion. She'd been in seclusion for some weeks, and had responded by smearing her faeces and menstrual blood on the walls. I liked her fighting spirit, and for whatever reason, she agreed to see me. To the alarm of the staff, she was sweet and told me why she shouldn't be kept in these conditions. It was hard not to disagree. 'I need a little bit of time to think about this,' I said to her, and so began a series of negotiated conversations between Zita and our team.

We all agreed that if Zita remained settled for an hour, she'd be able to spend the next 10 minutes outside the seclusion room. If she continued to manage without running off, throwing herself at the wall, biting or spitting at staff, then the amount of time out of seclusion would be increased until eventually Zita could stay fulltime on the open ward. Together, our team had decided to give Zita the opportunity to take responsibility for her behaviour. We'd been reminded of the notion that competency can be presumed until proven otherwise, and that it is specific to individual decisions. Moreover, vacillation when trying to make a decision is not incompetency but indecisiveness.

One of the aspects that I like about working with people with BPD is that the clinical situations I encounter, such as those narrated above, stretch me into thinking about treatment issues and approaches that I might not otherwise consider. [2, 27, 32–35] The idea of 'alternative ways' perhaps first really entered my consciousness when one of my professors recommended that I read David Dawson and Harriet MacMillan's *Relationship Management of the Borderline Patient: From Understanding to Treatment*, published in 1993. If there is one book that has continued to shape my clinical practice, it is this. [33] The authors, both doctors, argue that the typical response of physicians faced with a person at risk of suicide is to diagnose a disorder that serves the additional function of legitimizing compulsory treatment. Intrigued by their observation that people with borderline personality respond differently depending on how they are approached, Dawson and MacMillan developed a different stance.

To illustrate their thinking, they presented the case of a young man addicted to drugs. When those drugs were refused, he threatened to jump off a nearby bridge. The dilemma Dawson and MacMillan faced was this: in the long run, hospitalization offered the young man nothing useful, but should he jump, they'd face an inquest, during which they'd have to explain to their head of department, the hospital's administration, the coroner and, in their imagination, a newspaper reporter as to why they had not hospitalized a man so sick and desperate.

In an effort to resolve their dilemma, Dawson and MacMillan began a discussion with the young man. 'We don't want you to kill yourself,' they said, 'but we have no way of stopping you if that is truly what you wish to do. It is up to you. However, we'll continue to see you regularly.' The authors' rationale for this approach, which they articulate in detail in their chapter titled 'The Necessary Conceptual Leap', is that patients seek self-definition and resolution of their conflicts and discomfort through their externalized, interpersonal negotiation with others. Patients' presentation of self as helpless and incompetent elicits the already controlling, definition-imposing authority of healthcare institutions, which makes these people feel even more helpless and incompetent. They then try to overcome these feelings by gaining control of the situation through what they sense is the only currency at their disposal.

According to Dawson and MacMillan, 'There is a special kind of self-esteem and sense of power that must arise from being so chronically incompetent, hopeless and helpless, that one antagonises and defeats the best and brightest healthcare professionals.' [33, p.50] Recognizing that responses to others are socially constructed, they argue that while we may not be able to change the person with BPD, what we are able to change is our *response* to their presentation. Dawson and MacMillan's relationship-management approach is based on the premise that the person with BPD is a responsible, competent adult, and that we should respond to their behaviour accordingly.

This approach also underscores psychologist Marsha Linehan's work:

> [P]lacing primary responsibility upon the patient to change her own life entails risks literally of life or death that the therapist must accept if treatment is to be successful. If the therapist cannot accept such a risk and strives to keep the patient alive at all costs, a patient will inevitably fail to achieve the goal of a life worth living. Acceptance of the possibility that the patient may commit suicide is an essential requisite [34, p.947]

Drs Donald Schwartz, Don Flinn and Paul Slawson concur. They claim that effective treatment of suicidal patients requires removing those responses to these people that reinforce and enhance their suicidality. Instead, the responses need to be ones that encourage them to accept responsibility for their life. That responsibility must, however, 'be gradually re-accepted. The person with a suicidal character structure has become used to letting himself fall toward death as a means of coercing others into catching him. He must be helped to recognise that the treatment plan will gradually remove those catching arms, leaving him with increasing responsibility for not letting himself go.' [27, p. 204]

Requiring patients to assume personal responsibility, to be answerable or accountable for their actions, is an approach not formally considered in general psychiatry. It is, however, a matter much considered in law. The following case from Australia, *Bennett v Manly Council & Sydney Water Corporation*, showcases a judicial decision interpreting the role of personal responsibility. Glenn Bennett, a strong swimmer and champion triathlete, familiar with Manly Beach and its submerged concrete stormwater pipes, was swimming outside the designated safe swimming area. As he bodysurfed towards the beach, he struck his head on the pipes and was rendered an incomplete quadriplegic. Bennett claimed that the defendants were negligent in failing to indicate the positions of the pipes. The defendants claimed that Bennett was the sole cause of his own injuries.

The judicial reasoning that followed confirmed that the defendants owed a duty of care to Bennett and that, by failing to erect a sign or some other form of warning, they were in breach of that duty. Also not disputed was the issue of whether the risk was, for Bennett, reasonably foreseeable, given he had advised companions swimming with him of the presence of the pipes. The main debate thus centred on what type of duty was owed and, in particular, on what Bennett's personal contribution to the injury was. This matter was subsequently taken up by a review of the principles of the law of negligence by Justice D. Ipp. While mindful of the political and economic imperatives operating at the time of the accident, Justice Ipp recorded the following observations.

First, while the defendants may have breached their duty of care by not providing a warning sign, it was Bennett's participation in an unnecessary risk that ultimately caused his injuries. Second, a duty to take reasonable care did not mean a duty to prevent any and all reasonably foreseeable injuries, as some injuries are exclusively the consequence of a person's 'misjudgement'. As such, a warning sign would do no more than state the obvious. What Justice Ipp's report [36] acknowledged was that previous law had imposed too high a burden associated with duty of care, all but relinquishing the role of personal responsibility. The report recommended changes that imposed a reasonable burden of responsibility on individuals to take care of themselves.

This issue of personal responsibility is one that my colleagues and I have long discussed and debated. One such colleague is Rosemary Draper, a woman I worked with for many years. I always valued her quiet and thoughtful approach to others and to her work. During a workshop that we convened, she offered these observations:

> To take responsibility away from another adult diminishes his dignity and can be experienced as humiliating unless he can own that he is unable temporarily to take responsibility for himself. The only justification for depriving that patient of her liberty is the belief that she has regressed so severely that her adult, functional self could not re-emerge to prevent her from killing herself, or, very rarely, someone else. We cannot justify depriving her of her liberty just because we are anxious. We have to develop a skill to discriminate between our own anxiety and real uneasiness about a situation which must not be ignored. If one has behaved sensibly and reasonably according to good standards of practice, one need not fear the responses of one's peers or superiors when things go wrong. [2, p. 56]

In thinking now about how I could have further conveyed this important aspect of our work to our colleague (the young GP) on the phone, I've decided I'd tell him what psychoanalyst and professor of psychiatry Otto Kernberg said when asked how he'd feel if one of his patients committed suicide: 'I might feel sad, but I wouldn't feel responsible.' [37] I'd also refer the GP, and indeed any of my colleagues seeking answers to questions relating to personal responsibility, to Gutheil's excellent article on the medico-legal ramifications of treating people with BPD. [35]

FURTHER COMMENTARY AND REFLECTIONS

The above three principles in concert with the slow and considered approach that our team uses when working with people with BPD derive from our combined experience as health professionals. The principles did not manifest themselves overnight but rather emerged through trial and, inevitably, error over a long period of time. Today, our experience with our many patients tells us that these principles have cogency, that they do make positive differences not only for people who are suffering but also for practitioners such as ourselves who have struggled (and still do) at times to know how best to work with our patients.

Our first principle—understanding—relies on our feeling for the person, for their story. We must authentically appreciate that he or she matters, despite all that's happened. This ethos is characterized by a basic human response towards and respect for people. Its efficacy in terms of therapy cannot be overlooked. Of relevance here is the finding from experiments designed to determine the effect of different working conditions, such as better illumination, on worker productivity conducted during 1924 to 1932 in the Hawthorne Works, a factory near Chicago. This serendipitous, well-known and highly influential finding was that people respond positively when they think others value them. Worker productivity at the factory increased not because of the changes in working conditions but because the workers perceived those conducting the experiments were concerned for their welfare. This outcome was identified and named as the Hawthorne effect by Henry Landsberger when he re-analysed the series of Hawthorne experiments in 1950. [38]

In their review of literature on therapeutic communities, David Kennard and Rex Haigh set out what they concluded are the features of successful such communities. [39] These were democratisation, with every person in the community having opportunity to share equally in exercising power and decision-making. There was tolerance for a broad range of behaviours, even those deemed alarming and confusing by ordinary standards, an atmosphere of shared relationships and facilities, and an overall 'culture of living and learning and of honest enquiry into difficulty'. [9, p.2] In our experience, these features need to be present not just by design but deeply embedded into the practice of everyone in our mental health teams.

The second principle is linked to the first. Yes, the person matters, but not unconditionally. To pretend to the person that we know all, can cure all, love them all is dishonest. As such, when set within a philosophy of care, the respectful use of 'no' is a strong therapeutic tool because it *sets limits* not only for the person but also for the therapist.

According to Alvin Pam, 'The fundamental principle behind the how of limit setting is clear identification of the specific behaviours that need to be altered and equally precise articulation of the consequences if those behaviours persist.' [31, p.434] Limit setting becomes necessary under two conditions: when disruptive, disorganised, deviant or dependent behaviour presents a threat to persons or to the psychotherapeutic work; and in situations of chronic depression whereby the person withdraws altogether. [12] The usual strategies employed to manage these aspects of therapy have been ineffective more often than not, and the person's acting out is too gratifying or provides too much relief from the sometimes difficult work of therapy. Equally distracting for the therapist are the entanglements outside the therapeutic setting. Often treatment requires numerous contacts with family members, employees and legal personnel, each necessitating detailed discussion. Under this load, the therapist retreats, rewards or retaliates, all of which serve to further distract the therapist from the work. [30]

> We then encounter the thorniest problems in setting limits; management of acting out cannot be done with the patient's immediate consent. Although limits are designed for their long range best interest, patients usually suffer in the short term, resent and resist the intervention, and are angry at the therapist. Since limit setting is typically imposed against the will of the patient, one can expect that the therapist's approach will almost always be received by the patient as authoritarian measures designed to deprive, infantalise or punish. [30, p.434]

Reluctant to be seen as a disciplinarian, the clinician retreats. In order to maintain the patient in the treatment process as an active participant, limit setting may usefully provide the person with the opportunity to share whatever capacity they possess to understand the underlying issue and to move together with the therapist towards autonomy.

Those in the literature who argue for limit setting articulate several tenets. These include a philosophy of care focused on gaining understanding of the person and what they are attempting to communicate (generally indirectly) and the therapist having an overall perspective of therapeutic benefit clearly in mind and made explicit in terms of pre-agreed (with the person) long-term goals. [40] Also evident is our third principle, that of gently returning to the person's own ability to take responsibility for self.

This principle is the one that we and (very likely) other therapists grapple with the most because of its attendant risks. Thus, for example, the goal when treating suicidal patients is to reverse the process that has led to the reinforcement and enhancement of suicidality. [27] The responsibility for one's life must be gradually reaccepted. People with a suicidal character structure have become used to letting themselves fall toward death as a means of coercing others into catching them. They must be helped to recognise that the treatment plan will gradually remove some of those catching arms, leaving them with increasing responsibility for not letting themselves 'go'. With this thinking in mind, we can come to appreciate what Sabert Basescu referred to as the 'radical difference' between truly caring for patients and being responsible for them. [25]

Various other authors outline the practical aspects of limit setting. [30,41–43] When validating a person's distress and suggesting that limits are few in number, realistic and transparent, 'The therapist first points out that the maladaptive behaviour that is threatening the therapeutic process … then he or she delineates the limits which therapy can withstand. Finally the consequences are explained … the central element of the limit setting process is the formation of an alliance between the patient's ego and that of the therapist.' [44, p.73] Limit setting is akin to the caring but disciplinary role of parents. [44] Although giving in feels more like loving than limit setting, saying 'no' is an act of love. [31]

Gaining a deeper understanding of the value of the principle of responsibility and how to put it into practice also requires, we suggest, a re-acquaintance with what we consider to be responsibility's 'siblings'—rescuing, the emerging biology of BPD, and medication. These matters form the content of our next chapter.

Chapter 4

KEEPING RESPONSIBILITY'S 'SIBLINGS' TO THE FORE

Responsibility's siblings cannot be considered in isolation from one another. They are a tightly bound trio.

The matters that we discuss in this chapter—the urge to rescue, the biology of borderline personality disorder (BPD) and medication—are all mediated by our principle of self-responsibility. In encouraging our patients with BPD to manage themselves in ways that enable them to fully engage in therapeutic work, we constantly face the dilemma, as the stories in this chapter illustrate, of how much responsibility is too much.

Fearful of patients harming themselves, we rescue them, time and again, despite knowing that these actions are unlikely to change anything in the longer term for them. Rescuing can take many forms, including responding to every phone call they make to us, no matter when, offering higher dosages of medication, and readmitting them to hospital or respite. Or perhaps we make excuses for their behaviours because of evidence that BPD has biological (heritable) antecedents. We rely on medication, perhaps in the belief that it will alleviate the biological deficits or, if we are honest, because medication is an easy, expedient option. While we do not advocate that medication has no place, it can mask what is really going on for the person. Some medication regimens, as this chapter shows, are so extensive that the person is likely to be in a medicated state that prevents them from undertaking everyday activity let alone therapeutic work.

THE URGE TO RESCUE

One morning, some years ago, a long, detailed letter came off the fax. Each personally researched recommendation was sweetly phrased as a suggestion, but the precision and structure of the letter's layout held the possibility of its future use as a legal document. The letter pertained to 23-year-old Brittany, and it, like the one about Sue mentioned in the previous chapter, implied consequences if we kept encouraging Brittany to exercise self-responsibility.

However, given we'd not been having much success in this regard, I'd been wondering if Brittany actually had any confidence in her own ability to understand and manage her unpredictable moods. Her mother adamantly stated that Brittany could not do this, but she, her mother, could. Brittany sat colourless and mute in the background as her mother talked. I appreciated that Brittany's mother was understandably worried about her daughter, but could she be persuaded to relinquish her role, I asked myself as she paused and looked at me. Then another question came to mind: How hard would that be for both mother and daughter? I also sensed what they might be experiencing, as I too was struggling to contain my own anxieties about relinquishing control to Brittany—of not trying to 'rescue' her from her own behaviour.

In the remaining minutes of our session, Michelle (whom we met earlier) asked me about her next ECT treatment. Not quick enough at the time to change from a psychotherapeutic to a biological frame of reference, I blurted out the non-committal but consistent, 'Whenever you feel comfortable, Michelle.' However, after she left, I felt uneasy. This was ECT. And this was the first time Michelle had considered extending ECT out so far. Would she be OK? Should I ring her and confirm? What if her voices come back? What if her suicidal impulses return? I had to stop myself. I had to trust that Michelle could support herself; that I did not have to hover, like a rescue helicopter.

Jade, who'd been so settled, suddenly relapsed. Her voices had returned, she couldn't sleep, and she wanted to harm herself. Apparently, she and her husband had had a fight. The crisis team had taken her to our respite house for the night and told her that one of us would pick her up in the morning. But before the team left to do this, we discussed who should see her the next day. I suggested that it shouldn't be me. I was worried that if I, as her psychiatrist, saw her, she'd receive the message that the present difficulties resided in her, prompting a medication rather than a relationship review.

The next morning, Jade's community psychiatric nurse picked her up, confirmed there is no need for her to see me, and drives Jade back to her home. Until I heard from the nurse, I'd anxiously hovered, again like that rescue helicopter, not all convinced that all would be well. I should've gone, should be on hand, I kept telling myself. I needn't have worried, of course, but the temptation to stay actively involved, to rescue, undermined my confidence in my decision not to see her.

The urge to rescue others is a universal phenomenon, but sometimes we have to resist that urge in the interest of giving people opportunity to develop, to go forward. If we are parents, we know that toddlers need to wobble and sometimes tumble as they learn to walk. We will, of course, make sure that the environment is sufficiently safe so that tumbles don't result in injury, and we will comfort and dry eyes if a tumble does result in tears. But then we'll again stand back and let our little ones clamber to their feet and move forward once more. If we're teachers, we may need to be reminded that solving problems for students robs them of the opportunity to learn. And if we're therapists treating patients threatening suicide, our aim will be to help them gradually reverse the process by which suicidality has become a way of life. That means not rescuing our patients each time they falter. As with toddlers and students, the people we support need opportunity to gain the confidence that comes from trying, re-trying and eventually succeeding.

In a clinical setting, the task is to be both empathically supportive and to facilitate new possibilities of responding to suffering. Psychotherapist Edward Shapiro recalls being asked by a parent, 'What if my daughter runs away from hospital?' He said he could have offered two responses. The first would be to say that the daughter would be discharged. The second would be to ask the parent what they would do. The first response denotes the solving of an immediate problem. The second, because it requires a sharing of the difficulty and garners the creativity that strong feelings often engender, can lead to the uncovering of a previously undiscovered longer-term solution. [45] There is a tension between providing an analytic love for the suffering endured by patients and according a respect and understanding for the choices that people make as to how they will cope with their suffering. Peter Shabad eloquently expresses why this tension needs to be addressed: 'To provide love or empathy without this proper respect for the potential freedom for our patients, even when the freedom to act in perverse disregard to their own interest, is to convey a pity that only reinforces the patient's sense of victimisation and passive resignation to an unfortunate fate.' [46, p.603]

We hadn't fully understood how hard it's been to change therapeutic practice in this direction (and for many it is still hard) until we began to read the corresponding literature more thoroughly. The change in mind-set has been a slow process, occasionally encompassing trans-generational time, and it has been driven by a variety of interwoven social, economic, psychological and clinical factors. We thus appreciate as naïve the expectation that an anxiously hovering parent will be able to resist the urge to rescue just because a therapist makes one accurate observation about how their child will respond to a 'standing-back' approach. Similarly naïve is the idea that the maturing mind of the child, diminished by its inexperience in tolerating the disappointments of the external world, can heal because of one 'application' of that approach. [47] As we emphasized in Part One of this book, everyone involved in the therapeutic relationship—person, parent, therapist—needs time to bring about change for the better in themselves and to support such change in one another.

THE EMERGING BIOLOGY OF BPD

Research in recent years, such as that by Mayo Clinic psychiatrist Brian Palmer and Harvard University's Professor of Psychiatry John Gunderson and his colleagues, indicates a genetic predisposition for BPD. According to Palmer, BPD develops out of a neurobiological flaw that predisposes people to have a highly reactive limbic (emotional) system in conjunction with decreased capacity for cortical control of it. [48,49] Palmer states that the neurobiological flaw appears to be about 55% heritable, with environmental factors either increasing or decreasing a person's likelihood of developing 'full-blown' BPD. [See also 50, 51]

One implication of a biological basis of BPD for therapy has been to shift the emphasis away from blaming either the child or the parent for the behaviour and instead to see the person with BPD as 'handicapped', to use John Gunderson's term. [52] We consider the term unfortunate, because it implies helplessness, which we doubt was Gunderson's intention. The term handicapped is more correctly reserved to describe a person who, because of a physical or mental characteristic, is unable or has difficulty overcoming some social or environmental obstacle. So if we can indeed premise BPD as an impediment of this kind, to what extent *are* people who possess it capable of doing what we might expect of them and to what extent *can* they be responsible for their behaviour?

Let me try to answer these questions as follows. Although I (John) was considered 'bright' when I was at school, no matter how hard I tried (and perhaps I didn't try hard enough according to my physics teacher), I couldn't 'get' physics. I could parrot what I'd been taught, but not intellectually understand it. By the time I got to my penultimate year of secondary school, I realized I was better off doing geography! It seems that there is something in my biology, in my genetics, that has produced a brain unable to get to grips with the particulars of physics. No compulsion or inducement has overcome that seeming 'impediment'.

In similar vein, if biologically-based explanations of BPD do take precedence over psychological explanations, then the answer to the above questions about competency would seem obvious. But before we agree on this answer, let's consider a clever experiment conducted by John Monterosso, Edward Royzman and Stuart Schwartz. [53] These three researchers asked a large group of college students and suburban residents to rate the extent to which they believed people depicted in four vignettes were responsible for their given behaviour. Each vignette presented a different scenario. The first portrayed a man with a history of violent behaviour who repeatedly kicked a person in the head after they'd fallen to the ground. The second featured a woman who never followed through with her plans and who, whenever matters became difficult for her, moved on. In the third scenario, a man, long fascinated with fire, sets fire to a shack where, unfortunately, someone has been sleeping rough and perishes. The fourth presented a woman who, by her own admission, is obese.

Embedded within each of the four vignettes was an explanation for the respective behaviours, but unknown to the study participants there were two versions of each explanation. One version, pertaining to the first three vignettes, explained that the person featured had been found to have an unusually high level of a particular chemical in their brains, which significantly affected their behaviour and the behaviour of many other people like them. The second account explained that the person's behaviour was a result of their background, which was characterised by neglect, violence and foster-home placements. In the case of the obesity vignette, participants were told either that the woman had a genetic abnormality linked to obesity or that she had been raised in a home where food was consistently used as a reward. The study's participants were significantly more likely to excuse people if their behaviour had a biological basis than if they had experienced a difficult upbringing.

While biological explanations may be preferred because the condition can be treated with medication and/or surgery, such explanations have their blind spots, as an article published in the *British Journal of Radiology* in 1953 attests. The article's title 'Metaphyseal Fragments of Bone' provided a provisional label for what the author claimed was a new diagnostic entity. [54] 'For the last few years the writer has been interested in what appears to be a generalised bone disease of small children, characterised by multiple metaphyseal fracture-like defects. These are often accompanied by considerable adjacent periosteal or soft-tissue calcification that eventually leads to cortical thickening or deformity … [which] cause remarkably little general disturbance or pain.' The author then presented the case of a young girl:

> At age 7½ months, she was still well and using her left arm again. The haematoma at the left shoulder had absorbed, leaving cortical thickening. The metaphyseal defects were smaller or gone and the rib fractures united. At age 12 months her right elbow became swollen, without history of injury. Radiographs showed considerable periosteal

> calcification at the lower end of the right humerus, no doubt secondary to a small metaphyseal fracture, although this could not be identified. There was similar but lesser changes to the left elbow; metaphyseal defects had reappeared at the lower end of the left tibia (with periosteal reaction), lower ends of the femora and upper ends of the tibiae. At age 17 months she fell out of her pram and fractured the right femur obliquely. In plaster this united normally and appeared firm two months later. The metaphyseal defects had gone. At age 23 months she again fractured the right femur, this time without observed trauma, while re-learning to walk. It united in a month. At age 32 months: still very well. Curvature of the upper end of the left humerus and irregular cortical outlines of the humerus of both elbows; left tibia now curved in its lower half. New costal deformity due to a united fracture. Since the last examination there had been an asymptomatic fracture of the spine. Age 39 months: healthy looking girl. The clinical examination was normal except as follows: concomitant strabismus with left retinal detachment; thickening of upper end of left retinal detachment; thickening of upper end of left humerus; left leg abducted and rotated outwards during walking due to valgus deformity of left tibia.

Having excluded the possibility of a congenital indifference to pain and a bleeding diathesis to explain a tendency to early bruising, the author added these observations:

> This child has had multiple fractures and metaphyseal fracture-like defects. Most of these produced little disturbance and many were chance findings on x-ray examination. They occurred (with the exception of the oblique fracture of the femur) without recognised trauma. Some of the metaphyseal defects led to much cortical thickening. She was very well and active throughout. Extensive biochemical and haematological examinations were not illuminating; all studies were normal except in two respects: a bone biopsy showed an increase of osteclastic activity, although otherwise normal, and at some time the serum calcium was elevated. These two abnormalities did not, however, indicate hyper parathyroidism as there were no other features to suggest this condition and a mineral balance was normal. They may conceivably have been related to the remodelling of post-fracture deformities. [54, pp.577–583]

The alternative explanation for the child's physical presentations need not be spelt out.

Our point here is that both biological and psychological perspectives are needed to gain a full as possible understanding of a person's difficulties. [55] It was with this notion in mind that I recently wrote the following letter to the editor of a journal of psychiatry. [56]

> To the Editor
>
> Biological advances, including a larger than expected heritability, may raise questions as to whether the person with borderline personality disorder can reasonably be held responsible for, or realistically change, their communication styles.
>
> Some years ago, the theoretical debate of whether we are 'merely victims of neuronal circumstances' took centre stage with an elegant series of experiments. Studies suggested that electrical activity in the brain occurred before the person became aware of their intention to act, in this instance to move their fingers, and the question arose as to whether any of us actually has free will. Considerable debate, and criticism, has followed. Various writers note the complex, intersecting and overlapping domains of the brain, the body and the environment. That is, the brain, although necessary, is not sufficient to account for all the physiological and psychological properties that make each of us a

> unique person. They note in particular the difficulty for a neurone-alone system to adequately explain the feeling of being ashamed, of being able to forgive or to receive and accept praise. Neither does an electrical model allow for thoughtless, automatic and habitual actions or, because a person has an urge, or image or idea, that they will necessarily act rather than resist the impulse … 'Whilst creative and careful studies may demonstrate electrical activity preceding an awareness of the intention to act, the task of random finger movement that involved no deliberation is a far cry from the behavioural concerns or law.' In relation to the person who pulled the trigger, to argue it is not him but the neurones in his fingers, as one commentator remarked, beggars belief.
>
> Investigative techniques will undoubtedly improve and continue to refine neuro-cognitive differences in people with borderline personality disorder. However, it is unclear whether this will be sufficient in convincing the court that such a finding has been responsible for the behaviour which brought the person there in the first place. Instead, there will be a need to demonstrate in what way this specific deficit may have affected the mental capacities to inform intent. Further, in order to excuse responsibility, it must be argued that everyone with the same impairment is likely to behave in this way on each and every occasion.
>
> The future is uncertain. Rather than resisting biological advances, such endeavours can contribute to understanding. If neuroscience confirms clinical experience, we are on safer grounds, the corollary being that discrepancies should stimulate further enquiry. It has been suggested that all forms of therapy are successful to the degree that they have found a way to tap into processes that build and modify neuronal structures within the brain … [Thus,] the likely scenario is that the person with borderline personality disorder can have both neurocognitive differences and be responsible and able to change.

To my GP colleague, I would now say that biology is likely to be an important consideration when working with someone presenting with BPD. However, keeping biology in perspective is also important, particularly in terms of its interrelationships with guiding the person towards self-responsibility and prescribing them medication.

MEDICATION

I'd arrived early at the meeting on anxiety disorders. The keynote speaker was mesmerising. He came alive as he described his molecules, how they slotted themselves into select gaps, and how this process opened and closed channels, enabling calm to pervade the nervous system. He was sincere, genuine and passionate. However, as he spoke, I began thinking about an adage I've heard from time to time: 'When a person complains to their physician of the side-effects of a favoured medication, it's like telling a mother that their baby is ugly.'

Towards the end of this talk, the speaker asked his audience: 'How many of you prescribe benzodiazepines?' Everyone except two of us put up their hand. In this way, the speaker emphasized the point he'd been making throughout his time at the podium, namely that despite understandable hesitancies about side-effects, almost everyone prescribes this drug and do so because, in their experience, benzodiazepines help their patients. It made me wonder why I didn't, or rather very rarely, prescribed this class of drugs.

As I drove home that day, an early memory came to mind. It began with the phone ringing. I ran to it, picked it up, and knew something was wrong as soon as I heard the voice on the other end of the line: 'Is your mother or father there?' I silently handed the phone to Dad, who listened for a time before asking, 'Is there anything else?' A pause, and then again: 'Is there anything else?' His face was grim, but his voice calm. Very little seemed to unsettle him. He'd been in the war.

Dad put down the phone, and went to find Mum, who was in their bedroom. I followed behind. 'Michael's been in an accident.' Michael, on his motorbike, had collided with a car. Mum's whole face collapsed as she slumped against the bed. Michael and I were adopted and meant everything to Mum. She'd often say that she wished our real mother had known us, despite us protesting to her that *she* was our real mother.

We didn't have a car, so my father rang our aunt.

As we walked into the hospital reception area, I saw two young people off to one side holding onto each other. Perhaps they were the people who'd been in the car. I wanted to stop to say something to them, but I didn't know what. On we went, down the long, polished corridor to Michael's room. He was just lying there on his bed, alone, unconscious, his broken legs suspended, entangling tubes surrounding him. The room was silent except for the hiss of pressurised oxygen. I began to feel hot but was ushered out before I fainted. I was given a tablet: 'Just to help you sleep.' I don't doubt that this act was well intentioned. But it was that same act that deprived me of ever knowing if I could have managed myself through the immediate trauma—if I *could* have supported myself.

This memory was followed by another. I had severe asthma as a child, and many a time we had to ask my aunt to take me to hospital, often in the night. I was put on steroids and for the first time was able to dig the garden over for Dad! I remember always being frightened of running out of my puffer, tapping my pocket just to make sure it was there. I know now that I over-used it. At some point, our family doctor saw me and began to talk to me about emotional matters. He quietly suggested that I might be using asthma as a way of avoiding or perhaps solving problems. I burst into tears. His surmise was correct.

At one stage, I told Duncan these stories, which prompted him to tell me how his experience of medication had shaped his views towards it. As a trainee psychologist, he worked at a chronic pain clinic in Southampton. The clinic had a rule that it would only see those people who had not been referred to or who had appointments with other doctors at the hospital. This edict initially sounded harsh to Duncan; after all, who wouldn't want whatever medical assistance was available in a quest to escape the miserable experience of constant pain?

However, chronic pain by definition is exactly that and so is not a problem easily solved. The clinic therefore operated on a basic model, used in many pain services throughout the world, wherein the goal is not to search for a solution but to find ways of managing the experience. This approach encourages people to look at how they use their medication rather than to ask for more, stronger or better medications. It asks people to think carefully about their levels of activity and to make changes in how they behave to moderate the experience of pain. The clinic that Duncan was working at employed physiotherapists to educate people about how to stretch and take exercise regularly within their limits. It also asked patients to meditate regularly, sometimes on the pain itself. The clinic then started talking to people about the idea of accepting their pain, a concept that is generally hugely challenging for people in pain.

The plain fact was that people who believed they were one operation away from their pain disappearing would not invest the time, effort and energy in making this series of changes in their life. Why would they? It was for this reason that the clinic did not accept people who were committed to searching for an external 'cure' for their problems—people who saw their pain as the clinic's problem, not theirs. The team at the pain clinic understood that the tools, strategies and techniques that could improve someone's experience would only be effective if that person made the often considerable effort to use them, and use them regularly. The clinic's team also understood that they could only work effectively with people who'd reached a point where they were prepared to admit that what they'd previously tried wasn't working and that they needed to start doing things differently if they were to suffer less.

Discussing our experiences, Duncan and I agreed that there is perhaps little difference between the way that patients experiencing pain and people experiencing emotional suffering approach health services. It makes total sense that people want any respite they can find from their suffering. They (and we) do, of course, live in a society that tends to validate people's emotional distress as 'disease'. In turn, most of us have been conditioned to expect that any disease we encounter can be dealt with medically. We often find, therefore, that our patients (and their family members) want to believe medication will solve their problems. These people also typically want a 'biological' label such as bipolar disorder appended to their condition so they can legitimise the emotional experiences they find crippling and the behaviour they judge shameful. It is not surprising, then, that those of us working in mental health care teams can find ourselves reacting to people's efforts to escape their suffering by taking care of them. But in doing so, we reinforce their sense of powerlessness and reliance on others, thus driving them away from the central idea that the problem is theirs firstly to understand and then change with our help.

As Duncan and I kept talking, he reminded me of the situation in our clinic during the four years before I arrived. Throughout this period, our team had a series of locum psychiatrists, predominantly North American. Duncan said he wouldn't know how to measure how 'good' each one was, but not one of them practised their profession in the same way. Because of this, they gave the people attending our service very different diagnoses and very different messages about the solutions, including medication, to their problems.

One of these doctors, for example, described himself as a 'bipolar archaeologist'. He claimed that he could 'dig up' evidence of instability of mood in the people he saw. He re-diagnosed many of the people coming to the clinic at the time as bipolar (rapid cycling!) and prescribed mood stabilisers. All of these patients were thrilled with their new diagnosis and its associated neat medical solution. And they did improve—but only for a time. For the people in our team attempting to encourage their patients to accept their suffering, learn skills to moderate it and to look the origins of their difficulties in the eye (rather than engage in escape), the foray into bipolar archaeology was a disaster.

Duncan then told me of another experience. Not long after he arrived at our clinic, he sat in on his patients' consultations with another psychiatrist. This physician was an older gentleman, Duncan remembered, a bit of a rascal and very popular with our patients. He'd ask each person how they were doing. If they said okay, he'd leave their medication unchanged. If they said they were struggling, he'd increase the medication or give them an additional one. He seemed unconcerned by the impact of events in people's lives, and seemed to brush aside the notion that their responses to these events were probably appropriate or at least understandable given their way of understanding the world around them. He never asked them about the usefulness or success of their therapy as though this was somehow a separate entity from the challenge of successful pharmacotherapy. Although this physician was not as overtly destructive as the previously mentioned psychiatrist, it seemed to Duncan that he was missing an opportunity to present a coherent view of the person's treatment as a whole by modelling to them that their difficulties were a problem they themselves could approach, albeit with assistance.

Duncan paused, and then went on. 'I remember a particular patient from the chronic pain clinic,' he said. The patient, Duncan explained, was an energetic older man with chronic lower back pain. He loved gardening, but if he spent too long doing it, he would 'flare up' his back, as he put it, and experience a couple of days of relatively intense pain. He could manage it, though, by pacing himself, taking two-hour breaks during activities that were demanding on his back muscles. One such activity was mowing the lawn. Those of us at the clinic suggested that he mow half the lawn and then rest so he could complete the task without a major reaction. He looked at us with a degree of incredulity more in keeping with a suggestion of paving over the grass or moving to live in a second-storey apartment: 'Leave it half-mown? That would look ridiculous. I'd never do that!'

Duncan said he was flummoxed at the time by this man's inflexibility, yet had since come to realise it is commonplace for people, particularly those accessing mental health services, to have inflexible patterns of behaviour and thought. Invariably, these had served important functions earlier in their lives but were still being perpetuated in the present day despite the obvious cost to the person and those around them.

We currently have a patient with a tragic and quite remarkably unlucky experience of bereavement throughout her life. Life has taught her again and again that important people leave her, and she's learned to deal with this by limiting herself to two relationships, those with her husband and her son. This is all the closeness she can cope with because every time she's separated from them, she thinks it will be the last time she'll see them. She uses dissociation and suicidal ideation to avoid the pain of these separations and the deep undercurrents from her past that surface each time she is parted from her husband and son. Her emotional turmoil is clearly unsustainable.

These examples of clearly irrational and unhelpful inflexibility highlight the relevance of a simplistic medicalized approach to alleviating the suffering of such people. How can medication address someone's belief that a lawn must be mowed in one go, especially given all the underlying schema, derived from a lifetime of experience, that underpins that belief? How can medication make someone let go of a lifetime of loss and resolve the ocean of fear, hurt and sadness that is left? It can't, even though it might, of course, help the process. And it is this understanding that all of us working in clinical teams need to have so that we do not, as individuals, tell our patients different things. We need the courage to challenge our colleagues until we together secure a coherent understanding of an individual's difficulties that goes far beyond diagnostic labels. We can then give our patients unified messages about what will help, thereby acting in the same way that pain clinics work with people in order to help them understand and commit to doing what will make a real difference in their lives.

So here is the dilemma: medication can be effective, but simply viewing the patient's suffering as something that can be medicated away is not, for us, the long-term solution. This point is one that some patients themselves come to realise: 'As soon as I saw the doctor take out his prescription pad, I knew I couldn't talk to him about anything important.' [57, p.323] The extent of medication given to some patients diagnosed as having BPD, as in the following examples, makes one wonder how they would even be able, in their medicated states, to begin talking about anything important.

Jane

Antidepressants:
Amitriptyline 10mg, citalopram 60mg, venlafaxine 225mg, mirtazepine 16mg

Antipsychotics:
Methotrimeprazine 150mg, hloperidol 2mg, quetiapine 150mg, olanzapine 25mg, risperidone 1mg

Mood stabilisers:
Lithium 600mg, sodium valproate 1500mg, lamotrogine 200mg, gabapentin 900mg

Others:
Diazepam 4mg, zopiclone 15mg, clonazepam 7mg, phenergan 50mg, melatonin 3mg, prazosin 2.5mg

Kylie
Antidepressants:
Dothiepin 100mg, fluoxetine 30mg, paroxetine 40mg, citalopram 20mg, venlafaxine 150mg, escitalopram, nortriptyline 50mg, moclobemide 300mg, buproprion 150mg

Antipsychotics:
Thiothixene 30mg, methotrimeprazine 50mg, thioridaxine, chlorpromazine 400mg, haloperidol, trifluoperazine 15 mg, risperidone 4mg, aripiprazole 20mg, methorimeprazine 200mg, olanzapine 15mg, clozapine 350mg, quetiapine 800mg

Mood stabilisers:
Lithium 1600mg, sodium valproate 2000mg, topiramate 400mg, lamotrogine 12.5mg; combinations of carbamazepine 1200 plus sodium valproate 600mg as well as the combination of lithium plus carbamazepine

Zoe
Antidepressants:
Dothiepin 125mg, prothiaden 100mg, desipramine 175mg, fluoxetine 20mg, escitalopram 30mg, sertraline 200mg, clonazepam 1mg, alprazalam 3mg

Antipsychotics:
Olanzapine 20mg, quetiapine, risperidone, aripiprazole 30mg, clozapine, thoridazine 400mg, chlorpromazine

Mood stabilisers:
Lithium plus carbamezepine, codium valproate, lamotrogine

Medication regimens with respect to BPD are evolving, however, so that is another matter to be factored in when determining when to medicate and how to medicate. There seems to be a change in the wind, with an increasing focus on the biological differences between people who have and who do not have BPD. Given the unsatisfactory response to current psychotropic medications, the changing paradigms, including the use of opioids and oxytocin, may offer new treatment possibilities. [58] Nonetheless, prescribing as an intervention, whether for medication, case manager allocation or hospitalisation, remains a complex interaction involving the nature of often unspoken meanings, expectations and relationships.

Pertinent to this last point is the fact that some patients hold on to the fantasy that the perfect treatment does exist, and they are understandably loathe to relinquish that fantasy. Medication is an intervention that is immediate and specific in its effectiveness. Thus, not to prescribe may be perceived as withholding and a lack of caring, potentially reminiscent for the person of earlier life experiences. For the therapist, however, the withholding can be experienced as a refusal to be distracted from seeing the patient as a person. Therefore, if Michelle, whom we met earlier in this book, was to experience a sense of wellbeing without medication or ECT, she had to know that she could support herself.

In short, prescribing is a vexed activity. Treatment choices, adjustments and augmentation strategies can distract both clinician and patient from a psychological understanding of their difficulties. This situation risks strengthening the person's defences against change because they believe the only solution is external to themselves. If symptoms have become a person's armour, their removal is frightening. In addition, side-effects may serve both to confirm the patient's lack of lovability and to wound the prescriber, as in (to again use the aphorism): 'Telling a doctor his or her pills aren't working is like telling a mother her baby is ugly.'

Our understanding of the borderline experience will continue to change. The inherent dilemma of prescribing can be approached through an open and shared inclusion of the patient in developing time-limited, testable assertions: 'By making the patient a partner in treatment, the doctor emphasises and reinforces the patient's strengths as a person instead of his weakness in a dependent, sick role, thus opening up the door for more flexible, appropriate, response and responsible drug therapy.' [59, p.9] Changes in treatment approaches can thus be embraced rather than feared.

To my GP colleague, politely remaining on the phone, I'd say that I haven't had much luck with medication when working with people with BPD but I've certainly been distracted from the task by trying to add or subtract them! In more serious mode, I'd tell him that for many years I considered that none of the relevant literature supported the use of medication and so I'd continued with my preferred approach. It wasn't until I went to another meeting where those attending spoke of medication that would make a difference that I decided to ask my patients what their experience of medication had been prior to seeing me. Nearly everyone referred to me or seeking my support had been previously offered some form of psychiatric drug. They also said that the medication had brought about some improvement.

Accordingly, for the next few years, I continued to prescribe for people. Even though I was still left with that impression that it made little long-term difference, I had to acknowledge that, for me, prescribing medication had become an act of trying to control what otherwise was chaotic. Nevertheless, I wanted to see someone on a purely psychotherapeutic basis, and to find that they would respond to that therapy in the absence of medication, so having the experience of knowing they could manage without drugs. At the same time, I also became aware of how therapy sessions felt for patients on medication, with attention focused on this medication or that medication, this dose or that dose, and this side-effect or that side-effect.

And so I continued to struggle with the medication dilemma, at which point Duncan recommended I return to an evidence base. Back I went to the literature. Fortunately, the Australian National Health and Medical Research Council had just completed a very comprehensive review of the effectiveness of the various medications prescribed to people with BPD. [60] I know one of the authors, Andrew Chanen, and respect his integrity and reliability. The review confirmed for me that there is no specific medication effective in treating this disorder.

Around the same time, I met a new person who, unusually, had not been prescribed any medication until two weeks before she met with me. We chatted together, and she decided to try the medication for a little longer to determine whether or not it made a difference. The review included a table in their paper in which they set out what medications are being used to target which specific symptoms. This provided me with a useful format for discussing medication with her. Because she, herself, was active in this decision making process, I felt comfortable about her staying on the drug. I've since used the table to discuss medication regimes with other patients. Together, we sit, review what they've been on, what has been useful and what not. In so doing, we open up other suggestions, often novel. The point I am making here, of course, is that this process directly involves the person in their difficulties and in finding their solutions.

Mila comes to mind as I make this point. Over time, she'd been on many different medications, so as a team we elected to cautiously support her to come off each one. To her and our service's credit, Mila agreed to an inpatient admission for the express purpose of coming off medication. She did so without difficulty, even though we'd actually wanted to do the weaning more slowly than she herself determined. After Mila left, the inevitable pressures in her life again took hold, and she struggled. Gradually, we reintroduced those medicines that she herself found helpful. Given that Mila continued to be an active partner in this process, having shifted from the passenger seat to the driver's seat of her disorder, we all felt a lot more comfortable with the medication that she was on. However, she began to re-experience in particular the memories of forced oral sex, which caused her to vomit and dry retch uncontrollably. We explored different options, including having a chat with one of our American colleagues. He suggested ondansetron. He'd trained more recently than me, and had come across this drug during that time. He considered it would alleviate Mila's distress, so enabling her to continue her psychotherapy with Duncan. It did.

Jade, whom we met earlier in this book also came off her medication at one point, but then wanted to go back on it. Despite her requests, we supported her in her initial decision to stay off these drugs. We used a variety of strategies to help her manage her distress. However, one day, when we visited her at home, we found her again in considerable distress. She agreed to go for a walk with me. I felt that this approach would help shift her focus out of the home. She began to relax in this less formal setting and to explore the possibility of trialling a small amount of medication. After we'd returned to the house, her partner, supportive, felt that this decision was not unreasonable, and together the three of us agreed that Jade should take a small amount of quetiapine. The dosage was well below what she'd been on previously, but it did enable her to cope over the interim, and to re-engage in therapeutic solutions beyond just medication.

Similarly, with Mara, we found that a particular combination of medication was useful, with periodic increases enabling her to handle particularly difficult parts of her psychotherapy. Once she had broken through each barrier, she returned to a lighter level, and her therapy continues in this vein.

FURTHER COMMENTARY AND REFLECTIONS

Humans are unique in the proportion of total life spent in emotional and physical dependency, with individuation and differentiation being a phase-specific, developmental process continuing into adulthood. [47] As the child grows, opportunities arise for gradually developing independence—of assuming self-responsibility, which usually occurs at a rate commensurate with biological and psychological capability. Too little self-responsibility and the child may despise dependency, seeking refuge in the illusion of self-sufficiency; too much, and the child will be deprived of important opportunities to master their environment.

Rescuing is the extension of the latter, whereby parents not only seek to protect their children but actively intervene to solve problems so that their children don't suffer as they themselves may have. The literature shows that when these parenting characteristics are taken to an inappropriate degree, they can have long-term harmful consequences for their children, contribute to low resilience, a sense of entitlement and the increasing use of antidepressants and recreational analgesics. [47]

The same tension, of whether to guide or protect, is variously described in the clinical literature. By the time the person with BPD arrives at the psychiatrist's door, a considerable amount of learning with respect to self-responsibility has occurred, for both parties. Therapists and other members of the health care team may hover anxiously, striving to protect the person from further hurt. Others will have recognised that such protection may be doing the person more harm than good. Hard though it is not to rescue, we've found resisting the urge to do so is an important means of helping patients exercise self-responsibility.

Our changing understanding of the underlying causes of BPD also feeds into the self-responsibility imperative. Although we don't yet have a definitive answer, recent research suggests that that people's genetic (inherited) make-up may predispose them to respond to difficult situations with the behaviours characteristic of BPD. [48, 50–52] Hesitancy in setting limits, in requiring self-responsibility, may be rationalised on the supposition that the person cannot biologically be reasonably held responsible for or realistically changing their behaviours. At play here is the 'It's not their fault' argument. [61–65]

The issue of genetic predisposition also has implications for the role of medication in treating people presenting with BPD. To what extent is medication useful? To what extent should it be used? If medication has value, which types are best? When should they be used? When not? Answers to these questions in turn have implications for the exercising of self-responsibility and self-management within the context of therapy. And if this self-responsibility is sought, then the members of the mental health team need to be aware of the 'pros and cons' of rescuing the person when the 'going gets tough'. This interplay across responsibility's three siblings denotes how closely bound this trio is.

Perhaps the way forward that those of us working with people with BPD face when endeavouring to reconcile these responsibility-mediated dilemmas is to take the following considerations on board. First, we need to remember that therapy has developed over time through a variety of interwoven social, economic, psychological and clinical variables. Together, these contribute to the difficulty in changing this style of interaction.

In acknowledging this complexity, expectations of change can be realistically adjusted and principles of care shared. These include an awareness of what the consequences are for those in the care of the anxiously hovering parent, teacher or clinician. Second, we need to remain mindful that our role is one of engaged neutrality, a notion captured in the adage that 'the teacher does not love the pupil as such but rather the progress of the pupil and the work they do together'. And, finally, can we not, when grappling with this dilemma, 'understand the varying influences ... that lead people to do what they do and, at the same time, hold people responsible for their actions, thus according an all-important respect to their human dignity of having free choice?' [46, p.590]

Part Three: Putting Principles into Practice

Not everything that is faced can be changed. But nothing can be changed until it is faced—
James Baldwin

Chapter 5

'GETTING ON WITH IT'—TREATMENT-RELATED CONSIDERATIONS

One doesn't discover new lands without consenting to lose sight, for a very long time, of the shore—Andre Paul Guillaume Gide

In contrast to the longer psychotherapeutic approach that I'd taken to date, I wanted to try an approach that would engage people in focussed therapeutic work over a shorter period than usual but still encapsulate the principles discussed earlier in this book. We'd already been discussing the potential of this approach in the literature and at various meetings. We remain grateful to the people who were only too willing to share their stories for others and kindly asked them to sign the following consent form.

Consent Form

Firstly, thank you. We continue to be humbled by your generosity at sharing your story. We are hopeful that those who read our book will learn something that will be useful either for their own understanding or for the people with whom they work, as it is a collection of stories for the general population as well as for our professional colleagues.

Secondly, we wanted you to be sure that you knew what we were doing and ask you to sign this consent form. By signing, you will know the book is primarily about borderline personality disorder, that you have read, or had read to you, those sections that describe our time together, and that you have had an opportunity to make changes. The editors may make final revisions, but hopefully you will also trust their discretion and respect.

The other thing that we wanted to confirm with you is that no money has or will change hands between us: your gift has been your willingness to share your story with others for which we remain grateful.

Finally, we hope you have enjoyed being part of this project. It has taken a while, being nearly 72,000 words long, but we hope it is also a record that you do matter.

By signing underneath you understand the following key features:

I have read the material and agree with what's written, having had the opportunity to make changes.

I know that I am unable to withdraw consent.
No monies have or will change hands.
Signed:
Witness:
Date:

Although confident in the approach, we were still amazed at how many of people were happy to try the approach and then how well it worked. It was as if both of us—therapist and patient—had to get on with it. When I was in private practice, people were paying a lot of money to see me and were motivated. And when I suggested the approach, people not unreasonably asked me to indicate the chances of success. I told them there were no guarantees despite the fees, but then said that people who did have positive outcomes were able to say three things: 'I've got a problem. I'm part of that problem. I want to work on that part of me.'

In similar vein, it wasn't until we seriously began consolidating our thinking on the principle of responsibility that we came to realize the importance of people being willing to actively participate in their healing. Some people sent to us obviously did not want to be there, as I quickly found out when they first came to my room. I typically started the session by asking how I might help. 'My doctor sent me.'

'Aha. Do you want to be here?'

'Nah, not really.'

'Okay, let's leave it there then.' Most were astounded. I also advised them that because consultations with me are very expensive, there would be no charge if they didn't want to engage in the work necessary. People generally appreciated the honesty, and we either parted amicably or got down to the work, knowing that both of us were now serious about it.

This thinking about, agreement on and experience relative to our approach to therapeutic practice is indicative of how our mental health service perceives therapeutic treatment. Although our overall approach to treatment is informed by the principles discussed in Part Two of this book, we do not see treatment as a set of practices that can be unfailingly applied to specific types of patient presentation. Instead, we constantly identify, reflect on, evaluate and modify our treatment practices according to the factors and circumstances we encounter.

Sometimes, these modifications, such as framing psychotherapy sessions within a set timeframe, will be ones pertinent to the more global practice of our team. Other times, they will be ones that we, as individuals, because of the particular role we play within the team, decide to employ. My decision to be upfront about my preference not to work with any person lacking any semblance of interest in doing the work needed is a case in point.

The first story we present in this chapter provides an example of both these treatment-aligned practices 'in action'. Other stories showcase other such practices. Some of the stories are relatively short; some much longer. All say something about the learning relative to treatment that we gain from each person and our sessions with them. And all are followed by commentary and reflections on the hows and whys of the treatment approaches depicted. Throughout this chapter, which because of our wish to illustrate and elucidate in detail how treatment formulations develop and play out, is longer than the other chapters in this book, we implicitly explore the question of just what *is* treatment with respect to borderline personality disorder (BPD). In the concluding section of the chapter, however, we endeavour to provide a more explicit answer to this question, assuming such an answer is entirely feasible.

EVAN AND SAM

Together, Evan and Sam (short for Samantha) tell me of Evan's recent bout of extreme anger, during which he threatened to kill Sam. Evan's been in and out of prison over many years, his relationship with Sam coinciding with the longest period he's been on release—two years. Another physician has referred Evan to me with the suggestion that Evan may be experiencing fugue states. Evan's been leaving home for periods of up to three weeks, during which he assumes a different persona whom he's named John. Evan and Sam tell me it was John not Evan who threatened Sam. Evan is already on prazosin, prescribed by my colleague, when he comes to me, and it has helped dampen down volatility.

Evan's attempts at suicide began when he was age eight. The attempts, which have included cutting, hanging and carbon-monoxide poisoning, have all been prefaced by periods of considerable stress. There is the sad, familiar history of childhood sexual abuse, placement in various authority homes, becoming a street kid, and involvement in drugs. Evan's son Dustin has recently died of cot death, but Evan had already turned away from him, his daughter and the children's mother (a woman other than Sam). Evan remains excluded from both this family and his extended family, but interestingly has not attempted suicide over the past two years.

Some of the neurologists and psychiatrists who've seen Evan since he experienced a head injury when a child think his hallucinatory experiences might be schizophrenic in form and related to temporal lobe epilepsy; the others disagree. There is a long family history of criminality, bipolarity, schizophrenia and attention deficit hyperactivity disorder (ADHD). I am dubious, though, as to the extent these diagnoses can still be supported today. Despite all Evan has been through and despite the difficulties he has brought into his relationship with Sam, here are the two of them, adamant they want to stay together, and Evan determined to complete his first ever course of therapy.

As I listen to their story, Evan suddenly tenses. The hardness of the prison etches his face; his demeanour indicates readiness to strike. Evenly, I ask, 'What's happening right now?' Silence. Evan's facial muscles clench mechanically. 'I wonder if this might be one of those states you were talking about?' Silence. Then, 'John's telling me to get out of here—just walk out!' Another silence. 'I want to stay.'

'What were you thinking about just before John told you to leave?' I ask Evan.

'It was when we were talking about the course.' Evan tells me that when attending his local course for chefs, his tutor's tone of voice can enrage him.

'And, yet, here you are, able to stay in the room. How did you do that?' I notice Sam relaxing. The remainder of the session is relatively unremarkable; that moment of staying is not.

'Do you mind if I'm honest?' I ask at our next meeting, the second of the two I have agreed with the referring physician is needed to assess Evan and ascertain what might be possible. I find the question a useful one because it encourages people to listen and gives them the security to speak. 'There are various diagnoses for what you've been experiencing, but I don't think they're particularly helpful. What is important is that your difficulties aren't likely to be helped by medication.' Evan looks satisfied, but Sam shows agitation. I quickly move to clarify and reassure: 'It's okay to stay on the prazosin, but there is other work to do.' Again, Sam relaxes.

I make sure Evan is looking directly at me when I say, 'I'm struck by how you managed at our last meeting, Evan, and I'd like to continue seeing you.' His pleased expression reveals that he's been offered little of value during his life. 'Let's work together for sixteen weeks and then have follow-up sessions after that.' The couple nod their agreement. 'I do need to let you know, though, that the nature of the relationship you have with Sam may change as a result of the work we do.' They look at me.

'I'm sorry, Sam, I can't quite think of a phrase that doesn't involve an animal at the moment, but it seems that you might be a bit of a "mother hen" if you don't mind me saying so.' To my surprise, Sam agrees.

'I'm an early childhood teacher,' she explains. 'Children learn by doing and making mistakes. It's important that they have the opportunity to do so without being rescued.' Sam's open honesty encourages me. This is quite a couple, I think.

I turn again to Evan: 'The other thing, I want you to do, Evan, is stop referring to "John". You are Evan.' We talk a little bit about this. Evan gives an example: 'If Evan has a choice to walk away from his tutor or for John to kill his tutor, best that Evan walks!' I think that what he's trying to explain is that John provides Evan with a way of overcoming the moments when he wants to lash out at others.

I set the couple some homework. It requires them to list not only those things that Evan uses to protect himself but also those times when he's reacted in ways that differed from these usual responses. 'I want you to try and describe those differences,' I tell them.

Christmas is approaching, so it will be a few weeks before I can see Evan again. I stress to the couple as our meeting nears its end that because Evan's story has been 37 years in the making, its effects are not going to go away in 37 days, 37 weeks or 37 months. They voice their understanding. We set up some contingency support plans for the holiday period in order to avoid hospitalisation. I feel we've made a reasonable start.

After the Christmas/New Year break, Evan, Sam and I meet regularly. I listen for those ordinary occasions that wouldn't rate a second look for most people but were a truly different experience for Evan. 'I was like a little boy!' he exclaims during our first meeting after the holiday period. 'Sam's family had me for Christmas, and we went to the Marlborough Sounds. I kayaked with her nieces and nephews. It was awesome!'

He's done the homework I requested. The exercise book he hands me contains his pencilled notes on his life and what he's done to cope. Jail, for example, provided a place where he could go to block out the feelings he experienced on the 'outside'. As we discuss what he's written, he admits that despite enjoying his time away with Sam and her family, he still had destructive feelings over this period.

'So what did you do differently that allowed you to manage them?' No answer.

'What's it like being able to sit here now with these feelings?' I ask him.

'I keep being tempted to get up and go.'

'So what is enabling you not to?'

Again, he doesn't answer, and we leave it at that.

During subsequent sessions, we draw a 'map' together. It depicts embers in a fireplace. Each one represents a response Evan nearly always makes when he feels felt criticised or judged. We look at what lights up each of the embers. Tone of voice is one of them. We agree that Evan's means of getting away from the embers have included abusing others, swearing, going walkabout, abandoning his feelings—until he was, to use his term, 'rescued' by Sam.

Increasingly, Evan comes to understand his reactions as his way of surviving. The new experiences continue to offer a way out, but from time to time he still wants to escape reality, wants to be in prison again.

'There's an urgent call from Sam. Can you take it?' I'm reluctant to take direct calls because it risks sending the message that I'm the one to help the person rather than the person helping him or herself. 'Everyone else is out, including the duty worker.' I pick up the phone.

'Hullo Sam.'

'He's completely flipped out. I don't know what to do!'

'What's happened?'

Sam isn't able to listen, quickly overlapping my question with a plea: 'Last time they gave him something.'

'Can I talk to Evan?'

Evan is barely able to catch his breath between sobs. "I ... can't ... I .... can't ... finish ... the course ...' Caught off balance in the absence of the rhythm of the consulting room, I forget to ask Evan to look at his map, which I know he's folded and always carries with him. 'Which ember is being lit up?' is what I should've said. Instead, all I manage is 'I believe in you. Let's catch up at our usual time.' What I've just said feels pathetic, but Evan, with Sam, turns up to the next appointment having survived without medication, violence or walkabout. Once again, I ask the question: 'What exactly did you do that was different?'

Commentary from John

Evan's file notes were not extensive but they made clear he had been in forensic institutions for most of his life. The key material confirming why was there to see: an imaginary friend in early life, sexual promiscuity, drugs, son Dustin's death and, unable to cope, his return to jail. What seemed to finally be making the difference for him was the hope and possibility brought about by Sam and his acceptance and inclusion by Sam's family. He voiced his commitment to change: 'I want to be able to say I finally completed a course,' he said.

Over the time Evan and I worked together, the responsibility that he, supported by Sam, took for his mental health impressed me more and more. The couple's relationship changed; something they noticed. Evan's mum died, and they managed. Having decided he wanted to see his daughter, Evan completed preparatory courses on parenting, parenting through separation, and on being male, knowing that he might still not be allowed to see her, yet ready to accept the outcome of the legal process. When I asked Evan and Sam if they would give me their permission to write about them, they said they would be honoured. Their generosity humbled me.

Andrew

Andrew, nearly two metres tall, looks disappointed. 'Oh,' he says, after I've responded with a yes to his asking me if I know what happened last night. He's disappointed that I already know about the incident because this denies an opportunity for a dramatic recounting, something he likes to do. Nevertheless, after a pause, he decides to tell me anyway. He'd dowsed himself with gasoline at a petrol station before the attendant flicked the override switch and called the police. The faxed referral I've just received about him records that Andrew will do anything to get into hospital. He pauses to gauge my reaction. I decide to shift the conversation, and to watch him as I do. 'You know your old case manager's died?'

'Yeah, we used to have some real screaming matches when we were in the waiting room, yelling back at each other.' He can't resist a cheeky but charming dimpled smile. 'I had a certain respect for him, actually.'

I'd first met Andrew a month earlier. He'd been discharged from hospital, but had come immediately to the clinic, where he informed me had schizophrenia. 'I can't cope. I can't stop the voices. I know my warning signs are there. I've done all the things that I was told, but I know I need to be in hospital for my safety.' I wasn't entirely convinced that his conclusion was valid, but I told him that I'd give him the benefit of the doubt on this occasion. I knew the inpatient psychiatrist, a thoughtful man, who'd referred Andrew to me, and I was comfortable about readmitting Andrew under this colleague's oversight. Andrew visibly relaxes as he steps out of the clinic, pleased that the can return to hospital. His close-cropped hair and his puffer jacket, long, bulky and black, make his head look small as it emerges from the jacket's collar.

Andrew is discharged from hospital just before the weekend. And so begins a series of invitations, as we watch and decline further admissions. We watch and we wait through an overdose, a knife to the neck and reminders of a previous stab to his abdomen, of previous violence. Andrew uses the reminders to tell us he is dangerous and implies that if we don't give him what he wants (further hospitalisation), he might murder his stepchildren.

And then we receive the dejected, 'It's been nice working with you. I'm going to get a rope.' Finally, there is the gasoline. Ambulance, police, respite services and even his long-suffering landlady have lost their patience.

Because of this situation and also perhaps because Andrew's size tends to intimidate the people who come to his aid, I bring his referral notes to our weekly team meeting so that we can discuss if we should change our wait and watch policy and have a member of the team see him. There in the pages is a father who had no interest in Andrew and a mother who indulged him. He was bullied at school, and when he tried to protect a girl, he was anally raped. Voices since, offensive and mocking, claim he is homosexual. It's obvious that Andrew has always been on the outside.

Duncan, never convinced Andrew has anything other than a few borderline personality traits, comments on his lack of communicable distress and the similarity between Andrew's behaviour and a pattern he had observed when working with people with intellectual disabilities. Certain people who struggle to cope when they were stressed and threaten to kill themselves but with no real intent to do. They would then react to the significant and probably surprising (to them) response of their support workers who would summon crisis assessment teams and talk in serious terms about depression. Duncan suggests that Andrew, whose IQ is modest, may have simply learned to use threats as a way of making other people help him cope. Either way, Duncan argues, the principles of practice we've described earlier in this book seem relevant and therefore ultimately helpful.

Commentary from John

Concurring with Duncan's assessment, I hadn't wanted to see Andrew in response to his escalating behaviour, and the team understood this. Equally, they didn't want us to be exposed to risk. Andrew's arrest and hospitalisation following the incident at the petrol station led to a court appearance. During it, the presiding judge asked when a consultant psychiatrist had last assessed Andrew. Although our team maintains that people attending clinics staffed by a consistent team don't always have to see a consultant psychiatrist, we knew this point would be lost within a potential media furore should Andrew do further harm to himself or anyone else.

At a recent team meeting, we'd coincidentally been talking about another patient who was being re-referred to our clinic. The most helpful thing we could offer this person was our understanding that he didn't have the diagnosis that he'd held on to for so long, and that medication, including his self-initiated and family-endorsed increases in dosage to manage moodiness, was ultimately unhelpful. We concluded that our experiences with him pointed to how we could work as a team with respect to Andrew. It had become apparent to us that each time we agreed to rescue Andrew by agreeing to his hospitalisation after a bout of self-harm, his behaviour regressed in terms of increased acting out. We needed to arrest this pattern in order to convince Andrew that he could manage and support himself. The team also agreed that I would take the lead in working with him. Although Andrew's frequent attempts at self-harm concerned me, the confidence given to me by the team reassured me that I would not be alone in my work with this young man.

While the team fielded incessant requests from various agencies for Andrew to be admitted again to hospital, he and I settled down to business. When working with someone engaged in frequent self-harm, I try not to take any interest in what often become increasingly elaborate attempts. Instead, I wait for a particular shift or for an opportunity to acknowledge the person's distress.

With Andrew, this opportunity came when his landlady rang the clinic to say that not only had he poured gasoline over himself again the previous night, but he'd also wet his bed and soiled his bed linen with faeces. Her exasperation and concern were tinged with fear: 'You have to do something!' The statement is one our team hears frequently, and our response to it now tends to be 'so does the person'. However, in this instance, the response rightfully remained unsaid, and my thoughts focused in on the incontinence. That was unusual, not only for Andrew but also as a means of self-harm. From the landlady's description, the act seemed to have a malicious component. But I interpreted it differently.

The next time I saw Andrew, I said to him, 'You must be really frightened, Andrew, that you are literally shitting yourself.' Our team had been asking Andrew to do something new, to manage his experiences without recourse to hospital, respite or medication. Soiling his bed seemed to be a reaction to this. We had to be careful that we weren't pushing him into a corner.

I needed to go back a step. Perhaps hospitalisation represented a change from his father's uncaring approach. Andrew knew that we cared about him. I also wanted him to be equally clear that we wanted to work with him in the way that we felt was helpful. 'I disagree,' he said. 'I know what I need.' I felt the subtle provocation and threat, and didn't hold his gaze for too long. However, I did not back down from our earlier-determined approach to treatment.

'Perhaps we have to agree to disagree on this point,' I said. 'But I can't do something that I actually don't believe will be helpful. What I would like to do, though, is to see you weekly over the next sixteen weeks. I'd like to get to know you a little more, go through your old files, and perhaps talk to your family.'

The old notes were instructive in terms of providing greater detail than the referral notes about Andrew. At the age of 10, Andrew was told that he had had a 'brain virus'. He had been 'groomed' into homosexuality and experimented with it. The views of the neurologists and the psychiatrists who had seen him over the years conflicted. Yes, there was the polysubstance abuse throughout, but there was also a lack of consistently defined psychotic phenomena.

A useful review of his presentations in his notes had identified a pattern characteristic of people with BPD. Over 10 years, Andrew's efforts to gain admission to hospital had always occurred in the context of stressors. Moreover, Andrew certainly seemed aware that a mental health history was a useful mitigating defence for whenever he breached the protection order his family held against him. His family agreed.

As our team kept providing the boundaries to the possibility of Andrew continuing to engage in self-harm, he became more settled in terms of regularly seeing me. 'Wow, you walked here!' I said at the beginning of one such meeting. Getting to our clinic this way was something that Andrew had not previously been able to do. On a roll, Andrew began to tell me about the homework I'd set him at our previous meeting. I'd asked him to find out what was required in order that he might realise his goal of being employed to support other people experiencing mental health problems. He said he thought he needed to begin by stopping his drug-taking. 'I haven't used marijuana for two weeks,' he said, 'and the voices are less.'

'That's really impressive, Andrew. How did you do it?'

'I went down to that place you told me about. My friend was there. She's heard voices, too, and she told me that if you're going to kill yourself, you will whether you're in hospital or not. "You don't want to kill yourself" is what she said. "You're only doing it for attention. Your children will have a sixty-five percent chance of suicide because that's what you've shown them. If you can't cope, kill yourself. For fuck's sake, sort your shit out and grow up!"'

I was again impressed with what Andrew had achieved and that he had taken on board his friend's challenge, but rather than just be an appreciative audience, I asked him, 'What's it like—people like your friend being up front?'

'I could trust her because she's been through it,' he replied.

'Honesty seems important to you?'

Andrew replied by telling me that Gerard, one of our team's community psychiatric nurses, had recently 'lost it' with him, but he considered that important. I didn't understand. 'Well, I knew if he could stand up and say what he wanted to say, I could trust him.'

Gerard had been visiting Andrew regularly. Part of Gerard's role with Andrew involved liaising between him and the agencies with which Andrew inevitably intersected. Gerard is highly experienced, and with this comes an unhurried warmth and gentleness, but he nevertheless found this part of his work with Andrew frustrating and tiring. He fielded numerous communications from agencies who were nervous about following our carefully constructed plans directed towards providing Andrew with a consistent message that we would not respond to his self-harm threats by hospitalizing him. I have to admit, though, that we ourselves were struggling with this plan: the risk of not hospitalizing and then discharging someone who continued to report suicidal thoughts was too alarming and encroached on our clinical confidence, self-doubt unhelpfully emerging and unsettling the consistency of this message.

For Gerard, these difficulties coalesced into exasperation when he visited Andrew to administer his depot medication. A depot medication is one that is prepared so that it can be given by injection. The medication then releases slowly into the body over several weeks. Andrew unequivocally refused to take it. Uncharacteristically, Gerard told him exactly what he thought of Andrew's attitude. Andrew, taken aback, sat quietly for a few minutes and then agreed to have his depot, presumably because of what he told me about this incident. Some weeks earlier, in mutual agreement with Andrew, we'd discontinued all of his oral medications. We'd decided to keep the depot, prescribed for the original but ultimately incorrect diagnosis of schizophrenia until Andrew made the psychological transition necessary to begin the serious work of therapy.

The next time I saw Andrew, he'd had a difficult week, but he emphasized that he hadn't ended up in the police cells. He told me he'd wanted to test if his 'stockpiled meds' would silence his voices if he 'took the lot', but he'd managed to resist the urge, the reason why probably evident in what he then told me. A friend of his, he said, had taken an overdose not so long ago and ended up in the harbour, dead. She had BPD, he explained. He then paused before asking me why it was that she didn't experience voices and he did.

'Sounds like she was important to you' was my response. 'Tell me a little bit about her.' Andrew said he'd never had a girlfriend, but this woman sometimes came over to his place and knocked on his door. 'She'd flip out, but I'd say to the cops that I would look after her. She often stayed over and talked. She said she wouldn't kill herself; she promised. I felt responsible when she died, and it took a long time before I learned that it was her choice. I couldn't keep her safe.'

Andrew's opening up to me in this way created a space in which we could really begin to work together.

Stuart

Stuart is 41 years old. He came to our area from Christchurch after the worst of the earthquakes that began in September 2010. Although he's no longer living in Christchurch, he's continued to feel aggrieved by the quakes. He caused consternation in the community where he was living in Christchurch by acting out rather than talking out his distress. Since arriving in Wellington, he's threatened to jump off buildings and to cut himself, sending photographs of these cuts to various agencies, including government officials. What we particularly note about Stuart's actions is that he settles when he feels that others are containing and supporting him. He seems to have no understanding or belief that he can contain and support himself. He tells us he welcomed his few days in prison and visits from community police officers, who often shared a kebab with him. He felt calm during this time. But we consider these 'supports' as not sustainable because they do not develop independence.

We also learn that Stuart has been referred to various health services in Wellington, but often hasn't turned up to his appointments. However, each time he's been at our clinic, he's been pleasant, speaks calmly and is respectful. We acknowledge this politeness and, partly because of it, ask Pathways, a national provider of community-based mental health and wellness services, to provide additional support. As a team, we ask Stuart to complete various questionnaires and try various medications. However, despite a promising start in therapy, he begins to act out again. He sends us emails saying he doesn't want to come to see us, as 'it isn't working'. We agree, after an escalation in self-harm, to readmit him to hospital.

Our team regroups. We realise we've been temporarily distracted by behaviour and so have lost sight of Stuart as a person. We sit down with him again and talk. His life has been sad. Outcast from his own family and picked on and blamed for all manner of assumed failings, he has few friends. His difficulties in reading and writing were discovered only in the latter part of his school years. Stuart limped along after leaving school, protected by his interests in music, art, model-making and sport. However, on reaching his 20s, Stuart decided that he'd no longer 'lie down'. Being treated as he had been wasn't fair, and he wasn't going to allow himself to be treated badly again.

Stuart re-engages in therapy and begins to really honour this earlier decision. In contrast to his earlier visits, during which he blamed others, he's starting to see his own role in his life. For example, several sessions back, Stuart told us that the bank had closed his account because of his threatening remarks, which he said he hadn't made. But then he paused and corrected himself: 'Maybe I've been treated so badly for so long, it comes out wrong, and I said things to the staff that I probably shouldn't have.' This self-correction provides the opportunity for Stuart to increasingly see that his pattern of interacting with others needs to be understood within the context of what has happened to him in his past. He's starting to realise that he perhaps instigates fights in order to feel significant, and to test whether we do actually care about him despite such behaviour.

Commentary from John

By way of comment on Stuart's case, I present here the treatment plan the team developed soon after Stuart first came to the clinic. We circulated this to the various agencies with which Stuart was involved at the time. We also describe Stuart's initial reactions to the plan, reproduced here with his consent, when it was read to him some time after it was formulated.

> Treatment Plan
>
> In Stuart's words, 'Something has to change; I can't go on like this.'
>
> On the one hand, Stuart wants to learn how to live life differently and to be less dependent on the police 'rescuing' him. On the other hand, he feels that he is not able to do this and so needs containment. It might be that Stuart is increasing his threats, perhaps with the intended wish of either being hospitalised or returned to prison. It may be of note that currently this escalation coincides with the Christmas period when people often feel alone. The difficulty, however, as it is for all of us, is how to balance being cared for and being able to care for ourselves. The latter promotes independence.

> At present, Stuart has been offered regular weekly work with his psychiatrist, Dr John Little. It is in this forum that Stuart hopefully can begin to understand a recurring pattern of acting rather than talking about his genuine difficulty and distress. As a result, Stuart can begin to approach his goal of living more independently.
>
> Between these weekly sessions, Stuart may have contact with the police, ambulance, his GP, the CATT [crisis assessment and treatment team], ED [hospital emergency department] and Pathways. Each agency has its own procedures and protocols which they are required to follow. Accordingly, these suggestions may not be easily translatable to different agencies. However, they are offered from the perspective of mental health input and are orientated around being able to contain and support ourselves.
>
> We consider that, in the first instance, Stuart cares for his own injuries. Should he need to be seen by the GP or the ambulance, his injuries are to be attended to in a matter-of-fact way, without socialising. At this stage in therapy, Stuart may misunderstand such kindness as caring, but ultimately kindness promotes a reliance on others rather than himself.
>
> The police are in a particularly difficult situation when Stuart is acting out in front of them. The matter is further complicated should Stuart's charges escalate to the point that he is returned to prison. This only reinforces the notion that he is unable to support and contain himself. I do not have an easy solution for this dilemma. However, as with any member of our community, and a spirit of wanting to develop Stuart's independence through personal difficulties, he should be charged for any offence he may commit in the same way any of us might expect to be charged.
>
> It is helpful where there is consistency between providers. Please encourage Stuart to return to see his psychiatrist, to talk about his difficulties, and to remind him that he would like to change and that, for him, it can't go on like this.
>
> From a mental health perspective, we see deliberate self-harm as communicative rather than lethal. In order to avoid reinforcing unhelpful behaviour, and unless there is a significant deviation from Stuart's usual patterns, he should be attended to by ED and discharged home. He does not need to be seen by CATT, as the nature of his difficulties is familiar. If Stuart presents at a time when public transport is not available, he might wait in the family room or the waiting room at ED until trains and buses are running again. Although it might seem hard, taxi chits and lifts home only reinforce that acting out is without consequence. The way to avoid this is for Stuart to stop self-harming and to bring his distress to therapy.

I read this plan to Stuart shortly before Easter, apologising for the direct language it contained. I knew the plan was clinically sound but this didn't stop it sounding somewhat brutal when I read it to him. My apology, I thought, would provide a space for Stuart to respond. 'I'm not wanted' is all he said and left. I also knew that my apologetic stance was not necessarily commensurate with our encouraging self-responsibility principle. However, flexibility of approach is sometimes needed in order to achieve other aims, such as potentially starting a useful conversation between Stuart and myself. Apologising would perhaps soften the reality of the treatment plan for Stuart, so making him feel safe to comment on it. As is obvious, this approach didn't have the outcome I'd hoped for. To put it simply, the decisions we make with respect to treatment and therapy will not always have the desired results, and that is something we have to accept—and learn from.

On returning to work from the Easter break, I found that Stuart had been admitted to hospital during it. A colleague approached me, his demeanour apologetic: 'I know there is a plan not to admit, but I didn't feel as if I had a choice. He was still suicidal.'

'Of course,' I replied, trying to reassure him, but taken aback by the fact that he felt he needed to apologize. Survival requires adaptation, for therapist and patient alike, which means that plans, as I have just pointed out, sometimes have to be treated with flexibility. The incident left me reminded of my belief (wish?) that everyone in a therapeutic team needs to have the same understanding of treatment parameters.

Stuart was discharged the following working day, and we set up regular respite as an alternative to self-harm and hospitalisation. Stuart remained settled for some time, an observation that he himself made. But then he again was brought into the emergency department. By the time we received the fax advising of this, he'd been sutured, transfused and discharged, only to buy a cigarette lighter, burn the stitches out and start the bleeding again. The bleeding was particularly dangerous given that Stuart's heart condition had required surgical intervention and ongoing use of warfarin, a blood-thinning medication. Once more, emergency services returned him to the ED.

The emergency doctor who'd attended Stuart on this latest presentation and admitted him, rang me. He wanted to know if I could call in to the hospital to see Stuart. He was aware of my 'policy' about immediate availability in response to deliberate self-harm, but as our ongoing conversation made clear, he was also distressed by the situation. 'How can you expect me to just discharge someone while they are still suicidal?' he asked. Given his concern was heightened by the added danger posed by the warfarin, I could see his point. 'You need to make decisions that you are clinically comfortable with,' I told him. We talked about our team's treatment plan, grounded in our principle of self-responsibility. He could see my point. Eventually, I reassured the doctor by saying I would visit Stuart and sign off on his discharge.

At the hospital, I found Stuart lying quietly in his bed, a bag of blood suspended above him. After talking for half an hour or so, I looked him in the eye, and said firmly, 'You know I don't think admission helps.'

'Yeah,' he replied with resignation. And, then, an unexpected gift. His face lit up, and he tapped me gently on my arm. 'I've been wondering if I should ask you where my Easter egg got to!'

From the time Stuart was discharged from hospital for this latest bout of self-harm, his dramatic attempts quietened once more, which he was able to acknowledge through an appreciation of his own work in achieving this. But progress wasn't perfect, and setbacks occurred from time to time. Throughout, though, Stuart kept coming to see me and was honest in regard to these incidents. When our agreed period of 16 weeks of treatment came to an end, I had to accept what was and, more importantly, what was not possible. At our last meeting, I read and then gave Stuart the following goodbye letter. At the time of writing, we have been reflecting together over what might happen when we meet again in three months. For my part, I don't think I have been as honest as I could have been with Stuart and with myself. I need time to think these feelings through in supervision.

Dear Stuart

I thought I would write this letter to you as a way of summarising our work together.

When you first came to see me you, had been so angry with EQC, WINZ,[1] the police, the ambulance service and Mental Health Services that you felt that the only solution was to kill yourself.

As you began to tell your story, I became aware how sad life has been for you—always on the outside, with your family, at school and now as a grown man with few if any real friends. I was particularly touched by your comment that you didn't want to be one of those people who was found dead in their flat weeks after their death.

In your 20s, you decided, enough is enough. You were no longer willing to sit back but decided to fight for what you felt was your entitlement. You wanted to be significant. Some of this was successful. Defending yourself in the High Court overturned your original conviction for wilful damage. Some of this has been exciting, as you enjoyed the battle act of trying to outwit the police. However, more recently, it has led to further disappointment. Whilst you had felt you could catch your breath in prison or in hospital, this was not going to be a long-term solution and something had to change.

You have been pleasant with us, and in return Pathways came on board. You were able to reflect on what two completely different institutions, prison and hospital, offered the experience of individual staff sitting, talking and listening to your story— you mattered. You also began to shift from blaming others to seeing your own role. After the bank closed your account, you were able to comment, 'Maybe I have been treated so badly for so long, it comes out wrong and I said things to the staff that I probably shouldn't have.' And again you could see why someone might pick a fight as it would be someone else to blame rather than fixing it themselves.

You also helped me to understand that continually being turned away as part of our treatment plan for you served to rekindle your feelings of being unwanted again. This enabled us to think about you saying to us that you were hurting before having to show us you were hurting. As a result, we wrote to WINZ for some additional support. We didn't get it, but we were able to manage this disappointment, something I hadn't appreciated until I sat down to write this letter.

It has not been perfect. In our last session I recounted the story of a lady who changed because she finally realised that she might lose her husband and children, the family that she had always wanted. As I thought about her, I thought about how little you have to lose. I could see that at least contact with the police and Mental Health Services provided something, but as you yourself recognised, you can't continue to keep harming yourself, as a permanent injury is likely. There needs to be an acceptance that despite all that each of us has done, we may be left with a return to the original struggle of all those years ago, underscored by the question of 'Do I Matter?'

I look forward to seeing you in our follow-up. Until then, it will be a period of consolidation, where each of us can think back over the time, what we learnt, what remains and what needs to happen. I have enjoyed the contact and am particularly appreciative of the Easter egg!

With my best wishes.

---

[1] EQC is short New Zealand's Earthquake Commission. WINZ is the abbreviation for Work and Income New Zealand, an agency which provide employment services and financial assistance throughout the country.

Emma

'Run your hands down the sides of your chair all the while paying attention to what the chair feels like,' I instruct, trying to sound calm. Emma's eyes are glazed, and she seems unaware of my efforts to orient her to the clinic room. Some distant part of me comments, 'So this is dissociation.' I feel fortunate that recent advice from my supervisor is preventing me from being overwhelmed by the alarming reaction taking place in the room.

Emma's been referred to me after being assessed by colleagues, who concluded that she needed help to address symptoms of anxiety, especially in response to conflict with other people. During her assessment, she described great terror; today, with me and her husband Allan, who is in the room with us, watching on, she is experiencing it. The rational part of me reassures myself that 'habituation' will occur. But it doesn't. She shakes, she rocks. She wrings her hands and constantly seeks her husband's reassurance.

Emma returns a month later for her next session with me. Her terror manifests in the same apparent dissociative behaviour as before. 'Try and describe what you're feeling right now,' I encourage, a comment that only elicits more rocking, apologies and nervous laughter. The ever-present look of panic on her face does not abate. I try something else. 'I think our first challenge is to try and help you get control of your breathing.' It's a line I picked up from another psychologist when I was an impressionable trainee.

And so the session continues. Upwards of 30 minutes—*30 minutes*—are spent in my impotent attempts to reassure Emma that her panic will abate while simultaneously trying to reassure myself that it will. It does, but glacially. We are able to use the last 20 minutes of the session in constructive therapy, a little more such time in the following session, and so on.

Commentary from Duncan

A view of myself I hold as a clinician is that I'm good at engaging people. I can appear interested, trustworthy, accepting and ultimately a safe individual with whom clients can share deeply held personal information, if not horror stories. How Emma's anxiety shook these self-satisfied beliefs. The effect her panic had on me was significant. I found those lengthy periods excruciatingly uncomfortable. Even when her fear had subsided to a degree that allowed her to communicate, it could return with a mistimed comment, a glib piece of reflection—in short, one of my numerous errors in therapy.

I was also discomforted by Allan's presence. For me, patients' loved ones attending sessions bring an added pressure, and for a time I resented the standard placatory statement on appointment letters that offers patients this opportunity. I admit I enjoy the 'glory', if that's the right word, when wives, husbands, parents or children give the appreciative nod that appears to say, 'You seem to be interested. You seem to understand a bit about what is going on, and we're prepared to place our trust in you.' But during that first session with Emma, Allan's affirming nod was replaced by a worried, quizzical expression that said, 'What the heck are you doing with my wife?' That made it hard for me to control my own panic and maintain an aura of calm.

In retrospect, I realize Emma never again fully dissociated after that time in our first session. There was something disarmingly honest about Emma's terror. I also realize now that despite the therapy being at times uncomfortable in the extreme, there was rarely an occasion when I thought I didn't want to continue therapy with her. When supervising trainees new to the profession, I've begun to notice their tendency to make suggestions to mitigate people's distress, which is assumedly one of the goals of practice as a clinical psychologist. But alongside these zealous efforts, I'd like to see acceptance of the fact there is distress and, given someone's past experiences, this is inevitable. I therefore think that, although it was uncomfortable for me and Emma, there was real value in what we experienced. Emma was learning she didn't have to pretend to be okay. Once she had that security, she could start conceiving of describing the underlying reasons for her terror. I learned just how extraordinarily brave Emma was in facing this experience each time she attended. More generally, I think I learned not to fear distress in the person I was with quite so much and to trust the basic theory that as long as the environment (including me) remains consistent, the sensation eventually abates.

Jade

I've become alarmed by Jade's recent presentations. I began treating Jade according to a diagnosis of schizophrenia, but I'm no longer so sure. I keep thinking of something Sigmund Freud said: 'A thing which has not been understood inevitably reappears; like an unlaid ghost, it cannot rest until the mystery has been resolved and the spell broken.' A colleague quietly encourages me to take time to reflect on what's been happening. With the support of our team, I reconceptualise Jade's difficulties not as a major illness but as other struggles. Ruth, Jade's community psychiatric nurse, and I think that Jade's relationship with her husband is of significance. Both Jade and her husband are adamant that their relationship is fine, but it's difficult to imagine that recurrent hospitalisations of a young wife and mother of three children are not having an impact on their relationship.

Ruth and I decide to challenge this claim and are surprised at the reaction. Jade tentatively begins to talk out her doubts, while her husband begins to venture into the possibility that not all is as they claim. As I narrated in Chapter 2, I'd admitted Jade into a respite facility several days earlier in response to yet another deterioration in her condition. As Ruth and I drove away that day, we glanced back at Jade, who is smiling as she waves us goodbye, behaviour in sharp contrast to how she's just been. Her manner has the feel of someone who's gained relief and comfort from being visited and listened to.

Ruth, the team and I continue exploring what might be the reality of the situation over the next couple of visits. We also suggest to Jade that we can approach efforts to solve her difficulties in several ways. One is suicide, Jade's expressed option. We posit this as 'fleeing into madness' and suggest that working towards not responding in this way requires looking at her relationship with her husband more honestly and for the two of them to renegotiate it.

Slowly, over time, Jade and her husband tell us that they've been thinking about separating. He says he still loves his wife but given her inability to cope with housework and their children when at home, he's finding 'doing everything' (work, children, meals, housework) increasingly impossible. Jade says she's long been reluctant to share her fears and concerns with her husband, as this will only add to his sense that she's a burden to him. Her comment prompts an angry interchange between the couple, but it also brings several long-hidden matters into the open. From this point on, the couple, with our support, begin to explore their difficulties in terms of their validity rather than in terms of what they've each long perceived them to be. We also begin considering what these emerging understandings might mean for them in the long term.

Occurring alongside this reconceptualization of Jade's principle difficulties is securing practical support, through Pathways, for Jade in the home. This nationwide aid agency has just opened a branch in our area, and the household support the local team provide Jade is superb. They work alongside Jade, enabling her to regain confidence in her ability to do things that had felt beyond her. Over the next few months, the house becomes more organised and cleaner. Meals are prepared on schedule, and Jade and her husband at last have time to themselves.

Commentary from John

Jade continued to do extraordinarily well. She lost 16 kilograms in weight, and she and her husband now feel more comfortable in disclosing, confronting and talking together. They and members of our team today laugh together when we reflect on what made the difference for Jade. She is clear that it was the involvement of Pathways. She knew she was the first person in the region to have their input, and quips that all of three of the local team had come around to her place because they had nothing else to do at the time.

There was a moment, though, when she slipped back. I said to her that she couldn't, as we were writing a book about her! She laughed. Together, though, we began to unbundle what had happened once again. We reminded ourselves that her relationship with her husband was going through a difficult patch. He'd just told Jade he'd had enough and that she sat on the fence between reality and non-reality. Although distressed by this claim, Jade nevertheless found the ability to reflect on it. 'Stress pushes me over to one side,' she told us, 'and with support, I stay on that side.'

This acknowledgement was another break-through for Jade, and it was what prompted all of us to reconsider the truth of her situation. We were able to help Jade and her husband increasingly normalize difficulties in relationships so removing these as a reason for Jade to escape into mental illness, a situation that created a stalemate between them both. As to medication, Jade periodically drops back into the clinic for small increases in medication, which she takes for brief periods only in order to get her through bad patches. Importantly, even during these instances, she and her husband have continued to talk about the difficulties that not only they but all couples face in their lives.

Mila

When I first start working with Mila, I feel well equipped to help her because of my training in cognitive behaviour therapy (CBT) and dialectical behavioural therapy (DBT). Mila is initially receptive to my attempts to challenge her deeply negative and clearly irrational views of herself: 'I am evil. My parents saw it in me. Everyone does.' This is not, of course, how I and the rest of our team see her. We consider her to be a pleasant, very intelligent, gentle person. An example of this aspect of her personality had occurred just a few days ago. I was driving in the local community when I saw Mila out walking. Suddenly, she stopped, stooped and plucked a small blanket, covered in mud, from the gutter. Having attempted to shake it free of mud, she straightened it out and hung it neatly on a nearby fence.

'I thought it'd be easier to find if someone'd lost it,' she tells me during our next session.

'A bad person would've been unlikely to do that,' I say to her.

'True,' she replies. 'But it's because I feel I am bad that I do good things—to make up for it. I was always told I was a liar, so I never lie.'

'Let's look at what you've just said more carefully,' I suggest. Together, we reason that Mila will always feel bad to some extent, because memories of the appalling sexual acts inflicted on her as a child will likely never leave her. She might come to terms with them, but they will still be there. Also, cues prompting those memories are everywhere, which she herself realizes. For example, she reads voraciously, but nearly always non-fiction in order to avoid sexual themes. 'But some fiction is just that good,' she tells me, 'it should be read. So, for those books, if they have sex in them, I just put myself through it.' This comment is telling not only of her intelligence but also her courage and spirit.

I particularly want, at this point, to help her see 'bad' in terms of natural feelings of unhappiness and betrayal of trust, not in terms of her having courted this abuse or in any other way being responsible for it. We also need to explore her self-abnegation within the context of a family whose members taught her she is bad, within the context of the hypocrisy of people who sexually abused her as a child and positioned it as her fault, and within the context of a fundamentalist church whose doctrine makes it very difficult for its followers not to feel sinful and evil.

Commentary from Duncan

Mila is also extraordinary in that she was able to give us an extraordinarily detailed account of her history during her first assessment session with us, and although upset while narrating it, she coped. Our team took this as an indication of her readiness to engage in trauma work. With this in mind, I devoted time and energy to helping her develop DBT skills—mindfulness, distress tolerance, and emotion regulation. Although Mila expressed her willingness to acquire these skills, the work needed to achieve this aim didn't gain traction at first. She and I kept moving onto topics and discussions of mutual interest whenever I wanted to take the emotional heat out of difficult moments. Mila has a wonderful, offbeat, sense of humour, so we often used one of her favourite books, *Deeper Thoughts*, by Jack Handey, to bring humour and brevity to sessions when the going got tough. We'd laugh over such questions and responses as 'What is it that makes a complete stranger dive into an icy river to save a solid gold baby? Maybe we'll never know.'

But this seeming avoidance behaviour was not a bad thing because it allowed us slowly, together, to reach a point where we felt ready to tackle the traumatic memories head on. Typical of Mila, she wanted to begin by addressing her worst memory. This courageous and, in retrospect, somewhat extreme approach came to typify Mila's view that therapy should be challenging and upsetting if change is to occur. I didn't disagree with her at the time, and still don't. However, I've learned through working with Mila and others that irrespective of how willing a person is to face their trauma, they reach a point at which they are so upset that therapy, for the time being, becomes counterproductive.

The trauma sessions were inevitably hard for us both. What happened to her as a child—overt sexual torture—is truly terrible. Yet, for both of us, her detailed and repeated descriptions of it had value. PTSD, we agreed, is like having shards of glass in your mind. The work we were doing together (trauma-focused cognitive behaviour therapy) involved sweeping up the shards into a line so that Mila didn't tread on them quite so unexpectedly. It also quickly became clear that Mila could describe what happened to her, albeit with considerable distress, from an adult perspective. 'I never had words to describe what happened. Now that I do, it helps.'

What also became apparent was that the true reality of the horror of her experiences—of which there were many such—was that she could only interpret them at the time from a child's perspective. She described the searching animal that inexorably encroached upon her in the dark, penetrated her anus with unstoppable force, creating indescribable pain. She thought at the time she would literally erupt from within and explode against the wall. These mini-deaths, as she termed them, had no precedence. They were incomprehensible, seemingly inescapable moments of horror.

The literature on trauma work continuously stresses the need for a person to maintain dual awareness during trauma sessions. Awareness of the present moment needs to work alongside the memory of and the emotional connection to the traumatic event. I found Mila's ability to recall details of trauma and yet maintain her presentness remarkable. Spontaneously, and without having read it beforehand, she one day used the precise title of Babette Rothschild's book on PTSD: 'The body remembers.' [66]

Mila's certainly did. During her narrations, she'd move through intense and variable physical states as well as emotions. She'd become dizzy and nauseous. Sometimes, sweat poured off her. Despite these reactions, she stayed in the present, always able to respond to a question or move with a change of topic, introduced whenever I thought we'd gone far enough.

Something I didn't initially understand but came to do so as we worked together is the role that dissociative experiences were playing in her presentation. She'd experienced psychogenic trauma seizures for many years before therapy, but these never occurred during our sessions. The trauma work increased her understanding of what had been and was happening to her, so providing her with a much enhanced ability to rationally discuss her family's role in her distress. Previously, she'd been crippled with guilt and a sense of loyalty to family members, always immediately blaming herself for what had happened to her and her behaviour since.

Unfortunately, along with this apparent progress came increasingly frightening and bizarre experiences of feeling threatened. She described hearing people outside her house, planning to rape and kill her. Through the walls, she heard neighbours threatening to call the police because she possessed cannabis. They also derided her for being lazy. On one occasion, during a visit from a friend, she became so frightened she took an overdose to avoid being killed and attempted to convince her friend to do the same. While I felt her symptoms were trauma related and not a true psychotic state, this development was a truly concerning one.

At this time, our psychiatrist was one of the series of North American locums mentioned in an earlier chapter of this book. He was a kindly, older gentleman who, despite being a little misogynistic, was popular with patients. He threw a kitchen sink full of medications at what he perceived to be Mila's psychosis. In addition to the quetiapine, lamotrigine, venlafaxine and clonazepam he'd already prescribed, he added a very large dose of haloperidol. This had no useful effect at all, so he made an articulate case for ECT, which, to my now shame, I not only agreed with but was instrumental in guiding Mila towards. I was frightened that she would kill herself because of her intense fear of being attacked. I have long since made peace with the idea she may have chosen not to endure the grotesque memories of the past, but this was different, and so I placed my hope in medical interventions that proved ineffective.

However, Mila's determination, intelligence and ability to adapt won through. She hated the experience of the inpatient unit and quickly learned to 'reality test' what was or was not happening to her so that she could cope better at home. Around this time, John arrived and took his place on our team. With his support, Mila and I reasoned that, despite here having access to everything that psychiatry had to offer, all at one time, there had been no change. The rational scientist in Mila agreed that we had no valid evidence as to the effectiveness of the drugs she'd been taking to a greater or lesser extent for 15 years. Mila provided the driving force behind the decision to admit her to hospital as a voluntary inpatient so that she could come off all medication. Although doing this made little difference overall to Mila's presentation, it did demonstrate to Mila the need to take medication that helped her fall straight to sleep, thereby avoiding the semi-awake state that people with PTSD fear so greatly.

PTSD sufferers tend to spend their entire day striving not to think about past trauma. The mental effort this requires greatly fatigues them, so they start to fall asleep. As their conscious control moves aside, memories invade the still conscious mind in a way that is more terrifying than the unconscious onslaught of nightmares that occur during sleep. The support and encouragement that John and the team provided Mila while she was in the inpatient unit was an essential part of her healing because it gave her the message that she could take charge of her medication (and body). Mila's time in hospital helped us fully appreciate the value of what we could achieve as a united team using an agreed on approach to guide treatment.

Perhaps, my bias as a psychologist is showing, but from what I've observed, it seems to me that teams often contain physicians and psychiatrists who write prescriptions to alleviate symptoms, thereby inadvertently reinforce their patients' underlying hope that medication is the answer when research shows that it may well not be. Team members may then 'prescribe' talking therapy without taking an active part in assessing the person's readiness for this kind of work let alone determining if that person has any real appreciation of what changing might involve and mean.

My intention is not to be anti-physician, anti-psychiatry. Many doctors take a thoughtful and collegial approach based on evidence and understanding of the individual. I also acknowledge that medical training and the demands of modern medical systems shape doctors to make quick diagnoses. Moreover, health-organisation support for psychiatrists to do the interesting and important therapy that people so often require has dwindled in the last two decades. These thoughts are amongst those that encouraged us to write this book. We fervently believe, from our experience over time, that mental health care needs to move beyond the stereotypical psychiatrist in the lead role, seeing medication as their primary responsibility and giving 'talking therapy' a cursory nod. Team-based approaches have much to commend them. They bring with them the advantage of collectively supporting a person, of bringing different yet valuable and valid experiences to bear on what is happening for that person and of collectively determining what therapy might work for them. Team members also provide one another with the support that is so necessary for anyone working in the mental health arena.

The next phase of Mila's treatment was informed by the eye movement desensitization and reprocessing theory (EDMR) training I had recently completed. EMDR is a psychotherapy that focuses on disturbing memories with the aim of alleviating the symptoms of PTSD. Experience has taught me that although EMDR is often accused of being a repackaged version of cognitive behaviour therapy (CBT), the framework it provides for the treatment of trauma goes beyond the core tenant of habituation in trauma-focused CBT. A growing and reliable evidence base, which I consider need not be discussed here (interested readers can refer to the bibliography at the back of this book) also attests to the effectiveness of this therapy. What I particularly value about EMDR is how reinforcing it is for the therapist. The tangible way disturbing memories change in quality, often morphing into poignant, sometimes very beautiful adaptive symbols of wellness is a joy to behold. For therapist and patient there typically is no mystery to EMDR: it simply allows people to use both their rational and emotional resources to understand traumatic events and then resolve the difficulties those events generate.

Not so with Mila, however, at least initially. For her, EMDR heightened her emotional distress in relation to the memories. 'I make more connections because of EMDR' was how she explained this process to me. For example, she rapidly linked an episode of violent abuse to two other memories, the first of being overpowered and restrained by her father and the second of being bitten by a pig: 'The inhuman strength in those jaws was like nothing I have felt.' Although these connections heightened Mila's distress as she relived them in her mind, she was gaining an increasing understanding that the trauma within her trauma was a specific moment during an oral rape she endured when she was seven.

Mila battled on in therapy, constantly vomiting despite use of anti-emetic drugs. Her eating disorder worsened, along with the 'marked voices', one of which was her abuser, giving her graphic descriptions of what he planned to do to her. Interestingly, the frequency of her psychogenic seizures began to decrease. Around this time, I attended the EMDR Institute masterclass, without question the best training course I've been on. It helped me understand (how could I have missed it?) that despite the progress we'd made, Mila's responses as a child to trauma were again stopping her from going anywhere near a true connection to the memories and emotional states she'd fled from in order to survive. The training provided me with a much better understanding of her personality and a more sophisticated way of treating those parts of the personality that I now realized I had feared and therefore avoided.

So, our work continues. Five years on, Mila is still alive and still willing to try to change her lot. Working with her has made me learn and develop as a therapist. I'm sure, knowing what I now know, that I'd have approached my first months of work with her somewhat differently, certainly more cautiously. But I didn't know what I needed to know back then. Also, Mila has always maintained that trauma work gives her a sense she is doing something, which instils hope, a critical and rare commodity in someone who has experienced what she has. However, this said, if I had taken a more cautious approach, this hope might never have surfaced. Without it, I am certain she would have taken her life.

Some of you reading this account might wonder at—even criticize—the lack of a final positive outcome for Mila after five years of therapy. I'm sure some of you who are therapists would take different approaches to working with her. But these considerations aside, there is much to value in Mila's story. It highlights the challenging and technical nature of psychotherapeutic work. By showing what goes on behind the closed door of the therapy room, it belies the apparent superficiality of the term 'talking therapy'. The nature of the material and the challenges both parties face over often long periods of time during this kind of work are made transparent. The story also brings to the fore the importance of humanity in the relationships we have with our patients. With regard to Mila, here was I, a male, having a trusting and trusted relationship with a woman who has had so many debasing experiences with men.

Finally, this is work that is hard for any therapist to do alone. I have considerable support from a skilled team, active input from a psychiatric nurse, my own supervisor and external specialist supervision. There is also support from trusted colleagues and master therapists whose ears I bend whenever I get the chance. Without this assistance and encouragement, I know I would have given up or lost my way long before now with respect to Mila. With this assistance and encouragement, I know that she and I can keep on working together.

PHIL

Phil is a 31-year-old unemployed man who's been creating considerable disturbance in the small rural Australian town where he now lives. He's recently arrived in this community from the drug culture of a major metropolitan centre. His loud and aggressive manner accompanied by openly spontaneously voiced threats of violence and self-harm alarm the community as he wanders the streets. They avoid him.

The judicial court refers Phil to our mental health service for assessment. The man who comes to see us is powerfully built. He's wearing jeans and a black singlet underneath a knee-length cardigan. He has a leather mitten on one hand, long hair and earrings. The scarring over the ante-cubital fossa of his right arm is consistent with, as we later discover, injecting battery acid. His response to us is intrusive, threatening, intimidating. He thrusts his head close to ours, shouting, reporting multiple delusions and hallucinations within a clear sensorium. His speech is thought-disordered, a characteristic even more evident in the seven-page transcript of a tape-recorded interview with him that accompanies his notes.

These tell of a psychiatric history that includes a diagnosis of schizophrenia on the basis of thought disorder and also a family history of the same illness. However, the notes narrate a history of polysubstance abuse and of a drug-dependent mother who committed suicide. Phil's notes also provide evidence for both borderline and antisocial personality disorders on the basis of repeated attempts at self-harm that include threats to jump from buildings and intravenously administer car battery acid, unstable relationships and affective instability. His daily medication regime is complicated. It includes two-weekly, intramuscular fluphenazine decanoate 50mg and daily chlorpromazine 300mg, benzhexol 5mg, prothiaden 75mg, moclobemide 300mg, buspirone 60mg, and diazepam 12mg.

Phil's developmental history has been marked by emotional, physical and sexual abuse, multiple placements in children's homes, conduct disorder and a forensic history of drunk and disorderly behaviour, theft, wilful damage to a police car and a five-month prison term for assaulting police officers. His medical history includes infective endocarditis with cardiac complications and noncompliance to antibiotic prophylaxis.

In the preceding six months, Phil has experienced four admissions to different hospitals, each stay lasting two weeks on average. He's also experienced interstate admissions ranging in duration from 3 to 18 months. As an inpatient, Phil's behaviour is characterised by angry outbursts, threats to kill himself if he doesn't receive immediate medication, and absconding. He 'plays' staff off against one another by telling one staff member that another suggested or said something different from what the staff member is telling him now. He also takes on the concerns of other patients, particularly women with histories similar to his own.

During his most recent hospitalisations, he was managed in high-dependency areas with repeated seclusion. At times when not in seclusion, he appeared settled, expressing a wish to change and admitting to feelings of sadness. No features consistent of a mood disorder are reported in his notes, and his eating, drinking and sleeping are all within normal boundaries.

Over the eight months after we first meet Phil, a member of our team sees him weekly, although a community psychiatric nurse, David, provides his principal care. I review Phil's progress fortnightly and then monthly. Our management approach focuses on addressing Phil's immediate problems by facilitating rather than distancing his contact with his community, rationalising his medication and avoiding hospitalisation. Referrals to social services lead to Phil securing appropriate accommodation and inter-state transference of welfare benefits. On Phil's request, arrangements are made for him to join a gymnasium and adult literacy classes. We inform the local police and general practitioners of our overall management plan and treatment strategy for Phil.

The opportunities we give Phil at this time to vent his understandable anger reduce the intensity and frequency of his threats. His regular attendance at the gym also seems to help. His lesser interest in the adult literacy classes makes for erratic attendance at these, however. In the meantime, we refrain from addressing the more irrational beliefs he keeps voicing. We also agree not to focus on his experiences, both past and present, for the time being. When a staff member with whom Phil has the most regular contact arranges to take leave, we discuss this with Phil well in advance and reassure him by telling him that another team member will be working with him, and that she will continue our agreed-on management approach. This person is someone he'd met sometime previously and who is familiar with his case.

Phil becomes more stable, and there are no further hospital admissions. After we discuss the matter with Phil, he agrees to us reducing and rationalizing his medication. This approach involves a gradual stopping of chlorpromazine and buspirone and reductions of fluphenazine decanoate to 25mg twice weekly and diazepam and benztropine to 5 and 4mg per day, respectively. He elects for his 300mg of moclobemide to remain unchanged.

But then we begin hearing of crisis-based incidents in the community involving Phil. One crisis in particular has the police asking for Phil's involuntary admission to hospital, but I choose not to do this. Phil, surprised at this, manages until the situation defuses. However, he later argues that I don't appreciate how difficult it is for him in the community; he can't guarantee there will be no more such crises. As a consequence, we develop, in collaboration with Phil, a strategy for managing subsequent crises. We give him a metaphorical voucher for five inpatient days over the next 12 months, which means he can choose whether or not an admission is essential for him. He can also contact his community nurse at times of crises so that together they can explore and use community-based strategies as an alternative to hospitalization. Should Phil choose to use his voucher, however, he will not be admitted until the following day. We introduce this delay to allow for the practicalities of transportation from his rural accommodation. However, the delay also provides a further opportunity for him to manage in the community setting and to avoid the inappropriate reinforcement of crisis admissions.

Two months later, on hearing of a friend's death, Phil again becomes suicidal. Considering himself no longer able to manage in the community, he seeks hospital admission via the voucher system. Although he has managed in the community when previously experiencing a similar level of distress, the hospital 'redeems' his voucher. We wonder if he is testing the voucher arrangement. After two days, Phil leaves the hospital. His leaving coincides with a weekend when there is little organized activity on the ward and also with a further reduction in his medication, which includes the eventual stopping of moclobemide. Having reviewed Phil when he said he wanted to leave the hospital, I discharged him home on fluphenazine 25mg twice weekly and benztropine 2mg and diazepam 5mg daily.

Five more months go by, during which Phil makes no more effort to redeem his voucher. When he fails to keep his next appointment with us, we discover that he's precipitously moved interstate after a drug-dependent friend from the city visited him.

Commentary from John

My experience with Phil confirmed to me the importance of looking beyond the signs and symptoms of psychiatric illness. It would have been straightforward to draw the same conclusion as before, that Phil was simply psychotic, a danger to himself and others, and therefore requiring both medication and inpatient treatment. However, closer attention to his history of abandonment convinced me otherwise. I began to trust in my judgement that, while he was reporting unusual perceptual experiences, it was the behaviours characteristic of BPD that were challenging to the community and to services. It is possible for a person to have a major mental illness such as schizophrenia, as well as BPD. The thought disorder strongly evident in his interview transcript provided clear evidence of the former, as this type of disorder is something that cannot be mimicked or feigned. Nevertheless, I considered that there was opportunity for Phil to learn to manage his BPD behaviours. The voucher system in particular allowed Phil continued access to the supports he had learned to rely on but not in a way that was unfettered and reinforcing of his behaviour. It invited him to consider his part in the process and to ask the question 'Do I really need hospital as this time?' For the first time, he was alerted to the possibility of other ways of managing his distress.

Striking a balance between being honest with Phil about my understanding of his behaviour and holding the line in terms of his subsequent admissions ultimately led to a single, uneventful two-day admission in the following year and a reduction from eight to three different psychotropic medications. The dose of the remaining three was reduced by half. Phil left the area and we therefore never managed to understand more deeply how his detached, unloving upbringing had moulded his personality. Nonetheless, I was reassured his contact with our service had brought him closer to, not further from, some of the underlying reasons for his behaviour and distress.

Ros

When Ros's mother dies, her father returns to work the following day. He says he's already taken enough time off during his wife's short illness over the previous two weeks. Ros has already experienced a number of bereavements in her extended family, but her family never speaks of them, even immediately after each death. Her father's behaviour following her mother's death confirms for her that emotional expressions are signs of personal weakness and therefore shameful. The year before Ros's mother died, one of Ros's cousins, considerably older than she, repeatedly raped her when her family visited his. Ros tried to tell her family what had happened, but they didn't believe her. What Ros learns from these experiences is that she is unimportant, vulnerable (by virtue of the repeated rapes) and defective (because she must have done something to cause the rapes).

Then, the final straw: Ros's favourite cousin drowns during a picnic at a local river. This death, her mother's death and the prior deaths of other relatives tie into this learning. She thinks she is cursed because those close to her die, and she thinks she presents a curse to them because they die. She avoids new relationships, struggling to invest in the few she is able to tolerate. Every day, she fully expects them to die and leave her. For her, love has come to mean inevitable future pain. She tries to cope with her memories, sensations, and emotions completely alone, but they are now overwhelming her. Her hate is no longer enough to protect her.

Ros's presentation is entirely consistent with these experiences. She is hostile, anger being the one emotion she is comfortable with. More seriously, she is dissociative and dangerously suicidal. She constantly ruminates on a ceremonial planned suicide. It is the only way she can now see of escaping from suffering she can no longer endure.

Commentary from Duncan

Dissociation and fantasizing about death are the devices that Ros came up with to cope with her experiences of trauma. The bereavements kept coming, cementing the knowledge she acquired about herself, relationships, the world and emotion. The experience of rape wove into the fabric of her vulnerability, aloneness and self-loathing.

This description provides a brief formulation of Ros's presentation. A formulation is not a summary of a person's experiences, what diagnoses they carry and what medication they're taking. Rather, it provides an understanding of how salient events in a person's life uniquely affect them and provides insight into why a person presents with the problems they do. It creates an understanding of the psychological underpinnings of a person's experience and current behaviour.

A formulation provides clarity about what a person really needs to change if they are to become mentally healthy. In Ros's case, it was abundantly obvious that she required a means of finding peace from her turbulent emotional state that did not involve dissociating or fantasizing about death. She needed to explore and see the self-defeating nature of her vehement (albeit protective) rhetoric about emotions as pointless and life as meaningless. Dispelling her vast repository of unresolved grief required patient and careful attention. Her trauma symptoms would likely only abate with memory work, and she needed extensive support to prepare her to undertake it. Most of all, she needed a human being to patiently stay with her while she inevitably acted out her transference in therapy, in this case, her expectation that I would abandon her or abuse or trust. I and the team needed to show her through action and compassion that we would not.

Concise, formulation-based treatment goals such as those for Ros enable therapy teams to start responding to patients in a more coherent fashion, and to reference those goals each time setbacks occur. Ros twice took impulsive, significant overdoses between my sessions with her, the first of which resulted in her being hospitalised. She had let one of our team know she’d taken the medications and was angry at being admitted. She felt we’d betrayed her by responding in this way to her disclosure.

As a team, we had to weigh up at this time and thereafter the risk of her harming herself with the need to maintain our therapeutic relationship with her. We had to keep striving to let her actively understand we really were listening to her in a way she had not experienced before. She had to be reassured that we were there for her, no matter what, and would not abandon her.

The second time she took an overdose and told us she had done so, she understood our concern for her and did not interpret it with anger. Instead, she clearly stated that she did not wish to die as a result of an impulsive overdose. This statement gave entry to a conversation with her about how she wanted her medication to be dispensed from now on. We used the formulation to weigh the potential positive outcome of making minor alterations to her medication, acknowledging the danger that this focus could feed into her hope of a medical solution to her suffering. For us, as a team, the formulation helped us manage the anxiety that goes with risk tolerance. Once we agreed on precisely what changes Ros needed to make to improve, we immediately became clearer on what was moving her away from this goal and any iatrogenic role we were having in this regard. This clarity is surely the basis for clinically informed risk tolerance.

Mara

Kate, one of the psychiatric nurses in our team, asks me to see Mara, ‘Just so she can see who you are.’ I meet with Mara, whom we met in Chapter 2, twice in fact, carefully explaining the mode of treatment we might undertake if she decides to seek an alternative to her current commitment to death. John and Kate’s thoughtful management of her suicidal behaviour and vehement defence of euthanasia has brought her to a point where she can finally begin considering therapy. Having sat down for our first such session, she immediately says, ‘I can’t remember anything you told me when we first met, but it was good to find out who you were before we started.’

Our work together includes helping Mara cope with her long-felt terror in ways that do not include self-harm. She is haunted by memories and dreams of childhood sexual abuse, and experiences intense vaginal pain whenever these incidents become vehemently intrusive recollections. She has coped by staying at home, fantasising about being dead and deliberately hurting herself. She’s taken large overdoses of medication and packaged and labelled her belongings in anticipation of future suicide attempts. She frequently tells me and other members of our team or her intention to drive off a cliff near her home.

In the early stages of therapy, both the person and the therapist face a considerable challenge. The person, who has inevitably been abused by people who should have been trustworthy, must make a leap of faith in beginning to describe their inner experiences, often in a way they have never done so before. The therapist must show the person they are a trustworthy recipient of this information, without showing any strong emotional reaction in the early stages of the work likely to be perceived as proof that the therapist doesn't care, is appalled or simply cannot handle what they are being told.

And so the dance begins. When people at parties find out that I'm a psychologist, they invariably ask me if I'm analysing them at that very moment. 'Of course,' I reply, my face calm and serious. I then, with a laugh, make a flippant but light-hearted remark about the person's character. In actuality, I think I've become quite good over time at detecting people's emotional states, whether in the context of a party or of psychotherapeutic practice. But the former is, of course, a very different situation from the latter. When working with patients, we need to take time and care to understand what they have experienced and how that informs what they believe, how they act and how they feel from day to day. I constantly say to my colleagues, 'We can't sort out the problem until we know what the problem is.'

With Mara, my effort to be consistent in my relationship with her, especially to validate the suffering underlying her desire to be dead, is slowly rewarded with the information I need about her life so that I can form a coherent picture of her presentation. Mara tells me of her violent, unstable mother, and her amiable but generally absent father. She tells me, haltingly at first, of the sustained sexual abuse from her cousin, experiences she has kept entirely secret for the past 40 years. She comes to realise that her response to all of this has been an adept silence and an obsessive retreat into popular culture. She accepts that memorising entire movie soundtracks in fine detail might be an accomplishment but it is not helpful behaviour.

As time passes, she tells me of other responses, especially during her teenage years, which she describes as wild, involving parties, impulsive sexual behaviour and drug-taking. Reflecting on what she describes as her sexual promiscuity, she says to me, 'At least I was in control of it,' meaning that she decided when and with whom, in sharp contrast to her having no say or control over the abuse she experienced as a child.

In her early 20s, Mara began travelling the world, changing her name and entire persona—'I realised I didn't have to have a past, I didn't need to be me'—before being trapped back home by family illness. Her dormant PTSD symptoms came hurtling back after a sexual offender was placed at her work, arriving unexpectedly, just as her abuser had when she was young.

Once Mara has managed to tell me of these experiences, she and I can work to understand what they have taught her about herself, about others, about the world and about her own emotional experience. So the formulation—the psychological underpinnings of her behaviour—grows: in relation to her mother and abuser, 'People that I should be able to trust will hurt me'; in relation to emotion, 'It's bad to be upset, people will hurt you more'; in relation to herself, 'I'm a bad person so I deserve the bad things that happened to me'; in relation to the memories of abuse, 'I must avoid them at all costs because I'll die if I remember that.' Many more such statements follow. Put together, they explain everything. As the formulation takes shape, so too does her trust in me to help her complete even more challenging therapeutic work. While this early body of work doesn't have a profound impact on her symptoms, it does create increased and necessary understanding between us. I need to remind myself that at this point we are working at a surface, 'adult' level because Mara is not yet able to tolerate strong, confronting emotional responses to her experiences.

When we eventually broach the second stage of treatment—that of identifying the specific memories haunting her—her reaction has the force of fear: 'You want me to do what? No!' Asking someone who has spent their entire life trying never to think about certain things to come up with a list of the very worst is incongruous indeed. We spend weeks moving, inching, towards this goal. One whole session is devoted to the idea of a list, the next to the content of the list. At the session after that, Mara thrusts the list, folded, at me: 'You're not to read it! You're not to read it!'

We are planning on going into *Mara's* personal hell; most importantly, she needs to have at hand confidence that she'll be able to get out again. We therefore complete endless mindfulness, grounding and calming exercises, ably assisted by Kate, in extra sessions throughout the process. Kate also takes Mara on regular community trips, challenging her notion of threat and sense of vulnerability by showing her that she can do what she has previously found undoable.

The day arrives that Mara and I have determined will be the one on which we'll begin the most rigorous trauma work. Our aim is to reach the seam of shame that she always carries with her. I think the best way of dealing with her shame is to continue approaching her in my consistent manner and to look her in the eye when she tells me the sad reality of her childhood. *She* and I genuinely think we are ready. Unfortunately, the teenage part of her personality, still reeling from the repeated sexual abuse, swings into action. 'I can't even look at you. You think I'm disgusting,' she yells. It's astonishing to watch this cautious and reasonable (albeit frightened) person become a stroppy, unreasonable character who shows little inclination to think about matters in any detail and speaks only of the next overdose she'll take.

This attempt at direct trauma work brings home to me (and has been confirmed for me many times since) that someone can be very willing to take part in this most difficult of therapies yet be wholly unprepared for how their previously learned ways of coping can hijack them. I've found psychotherapist Onno van der Hart's approach to working with dissociative individuals with childhood trauma invaluable in this regard. [67]

Around this time, another of the movies in the *Star Trek* franchise is released. I know it will interest Mara. I reason that since I want to watch it as well, I can take *her* to it (and Kate as well so it isn't too 'weird' for Mara) and have my employer pay for the whole thing. My thinking is that if Mara can sit in public, in a dark cinema, for over two hours, it will be the ultimate piece of *in vivo* exposure.

The theatre is relatively quiet, not full, enabling Mara, Kate and I to sit away from everyone else in the middle of the theatre, a situation any therapist schooled in cognitive behavioural therapy would rub their hands in delight with. Although Mara is terrified of being in a public place, she manages and stays through to the end of the movie. Moreover, she is able to enjoy parts of a film she obviously adores and copes with those parts that engender fear.

I enjoy the film, and despite having carefully discussed the idea with my colleagues, I like that I have broken all the rules. But where is the consistency I worked hard to cultivate? What about the therapy room as a transitional and safe space? When Mara comes to our session the following week, she simply says, 'If you are prepared to spend time with me in public, I can't be that bad.' We also discuss two wonderfully poignant moments in the film that help Mara break through to true understanding that her responses to her trauma are entirely understandable.

The first occurred when Mr. Spock is accused of being emotionless and responds by saying that ever since his planet was destroyed, he's found it easier not too feel. This event in the film strikes me too with respect to Mara. This, I think, must have been similar to the planet-shattering aftermath of having your cousin rape you, causing the loss of all sense of trust, safety, innocence and cleanliness. The second moment in the film is when Captain James Kirk tells Spock that, for humans, denying one's emotion is impossible. Thank you *Star Trek*, I say to myself, for summarising the experience of complex post-traumatic stress disorder so succinctly.

During Mara's and my second year of work together we really start to hone our approach. Mara is able to keep the more unruly and dissociative parts of her personality in check, and she starts exploring fundamental aspects of herself. These include her inability to name emotional sensations, her lack of trust in others and her childlike fear that her abuser will 'get her' if she uses his name. In the last year of therapy, she really flies, making great changes and very rapid advances in understanding. Her symptoms change in perfect synchronisation with her ability to integrate rather than disassociate the material from her past.

Commentary from Duncan

Towards the end of our work, Mara and I had a session much like the last therapy scene in the film *Good Will Hunting*. As we looked at the very specific detail of one of the rapes she'd endured, she reasoned out that not understanding what was happening to her at that time was entirely logical given her age. And because she didn't understand, she was, in fact, innocent. Mara had known conceptually she was innocent for a long time, but this was the final, deep-level, visceral sense that she was not responsible; at last she was able to let go. 'I've just understood I really am innocent. I don't know what that means for me yet, but I know it's true,' she said through heaving sobs. In *Good Will Hunting*, the therapist character played by Robin Williams only has to tell the Matt Damon character three times that what had happened to him wasn't his fault, and he gets better. In reality, this outcome takes longer.

During this session, I was greatly moved and, unusually, did not prevent myself from tearing up. I would not have let this happen early in therapy, but I knew intuitively that it was right to show Mara my humanness, to let her see that my compassion for her was genuine. We talked what it was like to have affected her therapist so, and I think this was healing for her as well, as it showed she could reach out to someone else and support them.

Those of us working in psychotherapy talk about the people we work with a lot, but the effect they can have on us less so. More specifically, what we rarely if ever mention is the need for sessions such as the one just described with Mara that are truly redeeming, spiritual even in their hope and healing. I believe that it is these times that keep us working with these dangerous (to themselves), demanding and challenging people. Much of this book is devoted to how we thoughtfully corral our patients in a way that makes treatment possible. Having done this, we then have to do the treatment, and it can be long.

So, what then, is treatment?

Before endeavouring to answer this question, and as part of our conclusion to this chapter, we'd like to mention four people who improved and remained well for reasons that, for them, were not ones pertaining to formal therapy. When we asked them what aspect of their time with us (their 'treatment) they thought had made the difference, had helped them 'break through', each of them was clear on what it was.

Two of these people appear in this chapter—Jade and Mara. For Jade, the difference came in the form of the practical, home-based support of the Pathways team. There are 168 hours in a week. We might see someone for formal therapy only 30 minutes of that week. The Pathways team were at Jade's home every day of the week, including weekends, actively encouraging, modelling and supporting her. Their support enabled Jade to see what she had always been capable of. She was a mother, a wife, a person who mattered. For Mara, the difference was seeing the movie with Kate and Duncan, and her realization afterwards that if they were happy to spend time with her, she could not be so bad after all.

The third person is Christine. She had tried 30 different medications for her chronic pain, which she nursed within the context of her BPD. All 30 had no palpable effect. She made an appointment to see me (John). During it, she was adamant that she needed more medication. She sat bleakly, her nicotine-stained fingers hanging limply over the armrest. After some discussion, I said to her that ongoing medication was very unlikely to be the answer. Whether from anger or defeat, she took another nonlethal overdose soon after our meeting and was admitted to hospital. I asked the hospital not to restart her medication. This resulted in tearful recriminations, as Christine pleaded with me to replace her previous medication with something, anything.

Weighing matters up, I decided that medication would lessen her immediate agitation. I opted for a low-dose depot medication (a slow-release medication given by injection), an approach I've found helpful on occasion. Pharmacologically, a depot medication can occasionally dampen affective instability, with a reliability that is missing when oral medication is used. My decision, based on experience, was that the depot's true value for Christine lay in reassuring her that she was supported by a team who cared about her, hopefully making her more receptive to engaging in formal therapy. Ongoing administrations of the medicine and its monitoring would provide her with ongoing contact with our team and provide the team with opportunity to monitor her wellbeing. Some months later, Christine met someone. We didn't know how or who and we didn't need to. What we do know is that Christine is more settled than at any other time we've known her. Ultimately, Christine mattered to someone. The fourth person in this group is Sophie. She grew up with the distress and trauma of an alcoholic father, and has been engaged in psychotherapy. Sophie too has done well, and when asked what really made the difference for her, she is clear: Al Anon. This group, which supports families, provided Sophie with practical help and emotional sustenance throughout her therapy, reinforcing for her what she learned during these sessions: her father's alcoholism and associated abusive behaviour were never her fault, and her responses to that behaviour were her ways of trying to survive.

These four examples and the more detailed stories in this chapter make clear that treatment for people experiencing BPD is not a one-size-fits-all affair. The treatment approach or combination of approaches that we embark on will be as different as the people we meet. We do, of course, learn through our training, the experience and wisdom of our colleagues and our own daily practice that certain treatments can work well for certain manifestations of distress and trauma, and so bring them into our work. From there, we usually modify, 'tweak', even markedly change the chosen treatment in accordance with the person's responses to it. And when a treatment approach does bring positive change, what we therapists think has brought about that change may not be the person's perception. This is an important point for us to keep in mind because sometimes effective treatment can be as seemingly prosaic as providing someone with help in the home, as was the case for Jade.

To reiterate, treatment of BPD cannot be conceptualized or administered as one thing. As Rosemary Draper, a quietly spoken psychotherapist and colleague has written in her course notes for her students:

> Treatment of BPD doesn't refer merely to 'drugs and psychotherapy'. I would suggest that successful outcomes (and unsuccessful ones) involve the entire way in which an organisation relates to a particular patient. It follows that no single member of this organisation is worth more than another, and that "treatment" involves the way the receptionist answers the phone as much as the way the professor deals with the hospital board. Treatment is helping someone who might normally be able to deal with real estate agents herself and is currently so terrified of being homeless that she is frozen in inactivity. Treatment might be cutting someone's fingernails for her. Or fetching a glass of water for someone who could easily do it himself but needs to know you care.

When our team, while discussing these comments within the context of the principles underlying our overall treatment approach, asked her about the danger of creating dependency in the patient, this was her reply.

> Think back over your own childhood. If your own parents tended to be over-supportive because they were afraid to see you make mistakes or get hurt, you may tend towards doing too much for people or to rescue them. If your own parents pushed you to be independent too early, or pretended that they didn't care or because they denied their own fear of making mistakes or being heard, then you may tend to push people away or be too hard on them.
>
> Don't judge yourself when you do this exercise; don't judge your parents. Those of you who are parents have a huge advantage because of the day-to day training that small children offer in how to be a good support and how to relinquish that support as your child grows, develops new skills and finally tells you that your support is no longer required.
>
> Getting support just right, not too little, not too much, is a very difficult task. Everyone, every parent, every therapist has a bias in one direction or the other. You need to know your bias. Watch yourself. Be curious about the quality of support in your life—from your friends, your partner. Be curious about the support you give to your children, support you have experienced in the past. Don't criticise or judge, just observe.

Rosemary then made another important observation.

> If you were a tradesperson, you would spend time taking care of the tools you used in your job. That care of one's tools can be almost reverential. In this work, you are the

> tool. What you say and do is the treatment. Treat yourself with reverence, love and respect, and be observant.
>
> Remember to always develop a good internal support so that when things don't work out as expected, you can treat those times with equanimity, perhaps even laugh about it. The important thing is to learn from these incidents rather than feel humiliated or guilty. If things go wrong, it may be that you are too rigid or inflexible to allow the patient to make the mistakes necessary for them to learn.

Finally, she added, 'One of the things I love about this work is that patients really allow me to be inflexible, and the more inflexible I am, the more ingenious they become in circumventing my rigidity.' For us, the message implicit in this comment with respect to what treatment is and how to administer it is this: treatment is a series of approaches to working with patients that are grounded in medical empiricism yet always practised with the flexibility and humanity needed to accommodate human diversity.

Part Four: Reflecting on Experiences and Aftermaths

To accept one's past—one's history—is not the same thing as drowning in it; it is learning how to use it. An invented past can never be used; it cracks and crumbles under the pressures of life like clay in a season of drought —James Baldwin

Chapter 6

LEARNINGS AND OUTCOMES

In 1993, the mental health facility I (John) was working with was confronted with the increasingly difficult task of managing people deliberately harming themselves. In 1994, we began an organizational and community-based model of care. Five women who'd received an average of 14 different medications and had been hospitalised 12 times for an average total of three years were now in the community. Medication dropped to an average of 2.8 meds, admissions fell to seven, and the average length of stay totalled three months. Community contacts increased; caring in the community takes time and therefore money. Service-initiated phone calls increased from 2.5 to 79.5, home visits from 4.0 to 151.3 and crisis contacts from 0.8 to 17 per person. Of greater significance was the clinical observation that no new patient became as severely disturbed as these five women had been. Despite our hope of keep people safe from themselves by hospitalizing them, we'd been unwittingly making matters worse. [1]

This chapter contains contributions not only from Duncan, me and other members of the team but also from some of the people with borderline personality disorder (BPD) whose stories appear in this book. Several of the stories focus on the same person, thereby offering varied perspectives of that person and what happened to (or is still happening for) them. Much of what we've written in this book focuses on what we believe was occurring in our encounters with the people whose stories we feature. In an attempt to verify this belief, we invited some of these people to write their own accounts of their experiences. Their responses are illuminating, insightful and humbling.

These stories and the reflections in this chapter have in common two themes: learning and outcomes. As team members we learn from and support one another. No matter what our role in the team, every one of us in it learns from every encounter with the people who come through our doors or whom we meet in other facilities, such as hospitals. They, in turn, we always hope, will learn about themselves, why they struggle as they do and how they can begin to heal. Learning is, of course, an outcome in itself, but in this chapter we also take it to mean in the sense of what happens for people in the longer term who come to us for support. Naturally, our aim is for positive outcomes, but sometimes, as the first story, telling of a young woman's suicide, reveals, that does not happen. This, too, is something we have to learn to come to terms with as clinicians and therapists.

AB[1]

AB is 31 when she first arrives in our area. She's been referred by surgeons because she keeps ingesting foreign bodies, including knives, pens and cigarette lighters. Her neck is distorted by a mat of overlapping scars from her repeated attempts to cut her own throat. Her arms are similarly disfigured by traumatic nerve and tendon damage. Metropolitan hospitals state that they will only respond to her presentations conservatively. The police send written notification that AB should be hospitalised long term for her own safety.

However, two brief crisis admissions later, we admit AB for what turns out to be a three-month period. Intensive one-to-one special nursing and psychological input that include behaviour programmes contingent upon adaptive behaviour and multiple biological treatments for depressive symptoms are unsuccessful.

While she is in hospital, AB refuses to give us permission to discuss her situation with her concerned and supportive mother; she likewise forbids contact with any other family member. This situation makes addressing matters of risk and implementing a community-based focus of care extremely difficult. Nevertheless, we press ahead with garnering support from the Regional Personality Disorder Service. On hearing of this, AB immediately seeks discharge. Eventually, we decide we've exhausted all available therapeutic options and begin to accept that AB might complete suicide; further hospitalisation is unlikely to change this possibility. Graciously, AB accepts our request for a two-day period while we finalize accommodation and continuing care options. At the end of the second meeting, she thanks us for letting her go so that she can head away and kill herself.

As soon as AB leaves the hospital, we put the community plan into place. Teams are made aware of both the daytime and after-hours management plan. AB does consent to us providing details of the plan to the local ambulance services, emergency departments and Disability Support Services. Face-to-face and telephone follow-up continue. In addition, we continue to brief the chief executive officer, director of medical services and the hospital solicitors, all of whom have already been apprised of the community model. In all of these instances, we discuss no personal details.

AB survives the first week. Twice daily contact between Disability Services our team and other mental health services continues through the second week. There is considerable relief that AB has not killed herself. Self-harm attempts do occur during crises but are manageable and without readmission. The first month passes, then the second and the third.

One hundred and twenty eight days after discharge, a further crisis occurs. The same plan that's been implemented previously is activated. It involves a mutually agreed time for a home visit. At that visit, we find AB was lying on the floor, bleeding from a fatal cut to her neck. We call the ambulance but none of us can revive AB. Everyone connected with her case is affected; some of us cry. Most of us had liked her. We contact AB's mother, doing our best to express our sadness and sincere commiserations.

[1] We've kept her name (i.e., initials) as it appears in the coroner's report.

Commentary from John

We were a little uncertain whether or not to include AB's story. When I talked with Heather about the advisability of including it, she commented that the story represents a reality, that for some people, suicide is an option. It also emphasises just how serious BPD can be. We remain indebted to AB's mother, for giving us permission to tell her daughter's story.

Although we knew that our decision to continue working alongside AB in the community was correct, staff were also anxious. Did I listen? Did I try hard enough to understand? Was there something in me that didn't want to hear what she was saying? Will other patients trust me? Will they ask me embarrassing questions? Are you sure it was suicide? We knew there would be a coroner's inquest, a decision that would be pivotal in continuing, or being criticised, for what at the time was a departure from usual clinical practice. The report began, with these words: 'The record of investigation into the death of AB':

> From my study on the records ... I am satisfied that the deceased received clinical, diagnostic, medicative, social and practical care and management at the highest professional level from these agencies.
>
> I wish to record the communities' appreciations of the sustained report, the deceased was offered by these agencies; and I record the following remarks made by the deceased's mother in correspondence to the Coroner's office:
>
> 'I do not blame or criticise anyone for what has happened. It has been an extremely difficult situation. [The various services] gave her everything and made a commitment to support her in every way possible. I only have praise for them.'
>
> I record, also, my sympathy for [AB's mother] in the loss of her daughter, my appreciation of the harrowing role undertaken by our services and on locating the deceased in extremity, and my appreciation of the very careful and comprehensive investigation completed in very stressful circumstances. [68, pp.120-121]

From the People We've Seen

Michelle: 'What do I want?'

What do I want? I want something to help with the depression and something to help with the voices. I don't believe all avenues have been tried. I'm sure there's new stuff out now. Dr mentioned a placebo tablet. I was hurt and horrified and felt he thought I was just making it up. All in my head—make her think that something is happening. I know the problem with my overdosing is a big one, and I can't promise never to do it again, but there are ways around this. It's been really hard sitting here and knowing nothing was going to change. Yeah, there've been times when I feel better, which is neat, but I so quickly fall back into that hole where nothing matters. Even when I'm happy, I'm sad. I try to stay happy, but it just doesn't happen, and now I'm at a loss, as I'm sure you are too about where to from here.

Talking therapies, I have nothing against them. I agree they're a good thing, but at this time I feel with the help of medication it could help therapy be even better. Anxiety is really strong. Sometimes I can't even talk, so it's hard too. Sometimes perhaps I could have a larger dose, and just for this time while I'm adjusting. I don't know. I'm sick and tired of being like this, but know that if I go home (which is what I want to do at the moment to hurt myself), nothing is going to be the same, and then I'll work again and try again. Suicide is so much in my thoughts. Often the actions and plans are the voices. Yeah, amazingly enough I know the difference even though they always tell me everyone will lie and I can't trust anyone. It's hard to put them away, to stop listening. It's too hard not to believe them when it's so constant. I need help. If I didn't, I wouldn't have asked for it. For so long, I've been strong and put it aside, trying to do it all on my own. I know there are other things that meds can't help with; I'm not stupid. Right now, things are so bad I'm even confused. I'm waking early in the morning before I forget cos I do so quickly, and I can't blame ECT or meds, can I? It's just me. I feel stupid and useless. I'm gonna let Drs read this cos it's so hard to say.

Please don't think I'm lying, trying to get my own way. I just don't want to lose my family again. [I want to] be there, which I haven't in such a long time. I'm in constant despair now. Useless, all feels useless. The light at the end of the tunnel fades so quickly that's why I'm writing this [or else] all will be forgotten soon. Sleeping is so hard. Zoplicone puts me to sleep, great, but I'm awake three to four hours later, sometimes, even less, walking the floors, lying in my bed, trying to read. Morning seems so far away. Sometimes I'll doze, never for long and not restful. Sometimes [after] about half an hour I can fall asleep again but wake up and don't want to move—just stay where I am. It's such an effort to do anything but I know I have to and really really try when all I want to do is close myself off and die.

It's so hard. Sometimes I feel I can fly, do anything I want to do, then down I go so quickly before you can blink. I can't even seem to get those days back anymore. What am I doing wrong? Believe me I'm trying to be strong. I'm trying. Mood swings—so quick, so hard. It's got to be one way or another, but which way?'

Commentary from John

This contribution from Michelle was a letter that she wrote and then read out to me when she was in hospital. It shows the struggle she was experiencing as I was struggling to determine how best to proceed with her treatment. Our dual struggle also illustrates most of the principles we've put forward in this book and makes clear that applying them is often not easy, but nonetheless important.

I was actually on weekend call when the hospital where Michelle had been admitted phoned to ask if she could be transferred to the open ward. She'd taken the overdose soon after being discharged from hospital, and this time, she'd been admitted to the locked ward. I'd seen her during the week, the hospital staff having kindly brought her up country to our clinic. Still, I'm pleased to have this opportunity to catch up with her because I've been a bit fearful of having pushed my own agenda by asking the treatment team to wait before returning Michelle to medication or administering ECT. I'd suggested her overdose and readmission might've been a way for Michelle to avoid many of the difficulties that she and her extended family were confronting. The wait could let us watch over time. To my relief, I learn from the hospital staff that Michelle is beginning to 'warm up' and relate to others on the ward. She's done so in the absence of medication.

Both Michelle and her family continued to press for medication, however. I'd already had a discussion with Michelle about being uncertain and wondered with her whether we might try a placebo, neither of us knowing if the tablet would be active or not. This approach might then help us know if medication was truly helpful of whether her concerns were better understood as psychosocial in origin. If that were the case, the solution would also need to be psychosocial in form. Michelle was hurt, though. I apologised, and again wondered if I was still asking too much of her.

I discussed the conundrum with our new psychiatric registrar, who was also interested in developing a psychotherapeutic approach to people with BPD. To my surprise, she queried if I could continue asking Michelle to manage without meds when she was not a willing partner. I agreed, and then knew if I was to be true to our ideas, we needed to find a different way through what was becoming an impasse. As the registrar and I continued to talk, I told myself that if I accepted Michelle's request, I could console myself with the knowledge that we'd made some changes in my hoped for direction and that we could have another go at no medication in the future.

'Have you talked all this over with Michelle, though?' the registrar asks. The weekend duty call provided a nice opportunity to do just that. Fortuitously, the inpatient staff working with Michelle had just asked her to write down her thoughts. 'Do you want to look at them?' she asked. 'Perhaps you could read them to me,' I reply. She nods in agreement and begins reading.

The next day Michelle worsened. She was as I'd first met her, slowed up, largely uncommunicative and suicidal. The same uncertainty returned. Was this a biologically determined process? Was I asking too much? Had I become preoccupied with my own ego-driven approach? There was a lot at stake. Part of me was frightened. I decided to confer with the Regional Personality Disorder Service again in the hope of receiving some measure of reassurance. But there was still a part of me, almost obscured from view, where I'd been relieved when Michelle took the overdose soon after her previous discharge from hospital. What was she communicating by this reaction and how might that change the direction of treatment?

I was relieved to share my thinking during our Monday morning team meeting, after which I again, this time accompanied by David, went to see Michelle. This time she told of us of her fear of being discharged from hospital, as she thought her family wanted her out of their lives. In telling us this, she did what I'd done—shared her dilemma with those who mattered. There is a quaint Cornish expression, 'Bless her,' and it just fitted that day. She had relieved my mind and given me the confidence to continue to work with her psychotherapeutically. The team were again helpful. 'What would you like to be able to say about all this, John?' I told them that as Michelle's recent admission and presentation had unfolded, I'd become aware of the extent of my hesitancy, just in case Michelle became 'unwell' again. To help me find the way through I'd needed to share the dilemma with my colleagues. More importantly, I'd needed to return to interacting with Michelle as a 'responsible and competent adult'.

Ginelle: Groups and why I'd rather not

I'm very much interested in news or research relevant to me, but I'd rather not have to go to a group to find out about it. Personally, I loathe groups. I don't like being around strangers, and I don't like other people knowing my business. I don't want people I know from a mental health group coming up to me to chat in the supermarket, or talking to me in the waiting room. I know it sounds very unenlightened, but I really do not want people knowing me from a mental health angle. Even when groups have a specific, non-therapy focus, there is nearly always someone who will want to latch on when you very clearly don't want anything to do with them. The same thing almost invariably happens on the ward. I hate it.

Personally, I *never* want my parents or carers or anyone else to be involved with my treatment. The less they know, the better, so far as I'm concerned. Obviously this will be different for other people, depending on their circumstances and relationships.

Commentary from Duncan

I've never met someone who liked the idea of attending a therapy group and have met few people who, having attended a group, did not benefit in some way from the experience. For me, Ginelle's dislike of groups says much about the shame she carries with her. Shame is a less 'obvious' emotion we can easily fail to articulate to our clients who may freely talk about their anger, fear or hopelessness. Given the majority of people with BPD have experienced trauma and, very likely, been raised in an environment where emotional expression is seen as weak or simply dangerous, core feelings of shame are inevitable. If someone is unable to express how they feel or is punished for it, they learn they're unacceptable and therefore shameful. Statements such as Ginelle's create a dilemma: send her to a group to confront her sense of shame and hopefully find it isn't warranted or allow her to work individually to begin to directly address the feelings of shame. I'm not sure there is a one-size-fits-all answer.

Mark: Support in the longer term

The internet has opened up the world of international communication; people who would otherwise never have met can now discuss anything with anyone at any time. Interest groups that would otherwise have next to no members if bound by physical barriers today have international memberships, and have become such that a person no longer needs to physically be with the group in order to participate.

The same goes for international friendships—the concept of what constitutes a friendship has changed in the last few years. In the past, a friend was a person you could do physical things with, such as going out for coffee, or to a movie, or for a drink in a bar. These days your friends can be scattered around the world; – people you talk intimately with can be in completely different countries. It's been argued that these friends are not anything more than associates, but for some of us, these friendships are just as important as the friend down the road.

Over the last few years of spending an extensive amount of time online, I've developed friendships with an ever growing number of people who are interested in the same things that I am. These people come from many different walks of life, and are scattered across the globe. In this time, I've developed a kind of 'safety net', being able to discuss matters of mental health with others who've experienced the same things as I have. When once I would have had to go to group meetings with several people who may or may not have understood where I'm coming from, now I can discuss matters from the comfort of my home with dozens of people, safe in the knowledge that what I'm saying *is* understood.

This is why I believe that internet friendships are just as valid as physical friendships, and who's to say that an internet friendship might never blossom into a physical friendship over time as well? The world continues to get closer and closer together with air travel becoming cheaper and cheaper, so in time I may visit these internet friends, and it will be like meeting an old friend.

Commentary from John

I liked Mark from the moment I met him. He's bright, has a sense of humour and could make the necessary links between his past and his current difficulties. I first met him in crisis, with Mark describing derogatory voices, messages from the TV and radio transmitters incorporated inside his medication. He laughed when he told me he could take charge and switch the TV off. He also said that by taking more medication, he'd end up ingesting more transmitters. As is often the case for people with BPD, I observed an extensive and alarming medical history with a perforated ulcer at age 18 followed by a myocardial infarct and pulmonary embolus.

Mark was raped when he was 13 years old, and had been frequently hospitalized ever since. He tried to cope by blocking out any recollection, preferring instead an addiction to illicit substances, to sex and to prescribed medication. I was struck by how Mark would present himself at times when he'd been turned down for a job. 'I wonder whether you might have become "addicted" to mental health, Mark?'

Mark paused. 'Maybe I take overdoses to get attention,' he replied. Wow, I thought.

We've continued to see each other, monthly. From time to time, matters flare up. However, in general, Mark manages his distress remarkably well with a carefully developed set of specific mindfulness tasks that work for him. The main reason that I wanted Mark to include his thoughts in this book was for his own further development. He chose to describe his online friendship group, which he now uses as his preferential means of ongoing support.

Stuart: Being in therapy, the good and the bad

I found being in therapy had both good and bad side effects. At first, the therapy was monthly, which I didn't find helpful, as I didn't know what was going on. I knew I was unwell and was getting worse, but I was only interested in getting and trying medications to help with the downward slide I was in, and the deep depression and mood swings and thoughts of suicide. I thought this was the only way forward, so the doc and I had a few arguments about this. I couldn't understand why there was some hesitance there by him when some of the others I talked to on the ward were on five or more different meds. I just wanted it all to go away and be back to, at least, the minor depression I had before things started falling apart.

I never used to self-harm, and I don't know why I started or how it started. Both me and the doc lost our way a bit then. We sat down and openly talked about things. About how he lost sight of me as a person, and what each of us wanted out of the therapy. The doc offered to see me weekly. I knew things had to change. I knew I couldn't keep going the way I was. I would've either ended my life or been in prison, and the doc's openness helped keep me going back. If he'd come across closed-minded like some in mental health, I may not have kept on going, as I can tell when someone isn't genuine in helping or they're just there because it's a job, or they're not remotely interested in you, then …

Sometimes, though, I felt like I wasn't been heard and how bad the depression and other aspects were getting, and I couldn't understand why treatment options where closed to me, such as day hospital or short stays in the ward. I still believe that medication and short stays in a ward can help reduce the harmful effects of BPD. It seemed to me like others were getting easier access and more treatment than I was, and no matter how bad the self-harming got, I was just going to be sent home regardless of what I said or did, which added a lot of frustration and didn't help with the feelings of being abandoned and the dissociative feelings and the paranoid effects.

I think if a short stay in hospital had happened sooner than it did, it could've given me the chance to step back and reduce the stress and possibly stopped me ending up on criminal charges that could have affected the rest of my life. There where clear signs I was becoming more unstable, but whether the signs were being missed or ignored, I was ending up in the emergency department nearly two times a week, and there were lots of police call-outs. But I kept on being sent home without seeing CATT teams or a doc. All that just added to the self-harming and downward slide I was on.

If each self-harm or overdose was talked about openly, it may've helped reduce it and to prevent the pattern. It might've helped me find a different way of dealing with things instead of having it all put down to attention seeking, which it never was about. It was a way of deflecting the emotional pain I was in and a cry for help, and at times I just wanted to end it. I find that, overall, things need to change, as borderline is just as destructive as other mental health disorders and you're not all ways in control of your actions with angry outbursts that can happen without warning. It's unfair to be charged with something if you've no control over it.

When I finally got diagnosed with borderline and post-traumatic distress, it was a huge relief I finally had an answer, and I wasn't going crazy. So all this helped with therapy, as it gave it a better direction to go in. When the doc showed me a diagram of what was happening, it started to make sense; the cause and effect kind of thing helped me see the triggers of the self-harming and suicide threats. I also started to see the warning signs and how to reduce them. I learned more about the disorder. In the end, both doc and I had to be open and willing for therapy to help.

Doctors and others in mental health need to remind themselves and ask themselves what is in the best interest of the patient, as it is the patient and not them who's been affected by it all. They shouldn't always focus on their own views of things, because sometimes it means they get lost. Patients also need to be open to change. Sometimes things get worse while you're in therapy, and it brings up things you—I—didn't want to deal with, and it was hard to understand things sometimes, what had happened to me and where the therapy was going. But therapy can only really help the person to find more knowledge of the disorder. Better understanding will, in the end, help the person find less destructive ways of dealing with it.

Trust, honesty and openness of both doc and patient are the key to getting anything out of therapy. Without these, how can you learn or give good advice to help each other understand how it affects you?

Commentary from John

Stuart's letters to the various agencies he felt aggrieved by were filled with invective — capital letters and angrily formed sentences completed inaccurately through haste. He was genuinely pleased to be given the opportunity to describe his experiences in therapy, something that was evident in this change in his writing style. The letter above touched me (John) for its effort and honesty to communicate. What started as an effort to have our patients describe their experiences rapidly turned into a useful intervention in itself, allowing the people we work with to provide a more honest account of their experiences than seems possible in the therapy room. Stuart also showed me that, despite my best intentions, sometimes I couldn't make things better. Despite this, my asking him to give his account adheres to the principle of allowing ourselves to be touched by the people we see and to actively listen to their story without reflexively diagnosing or referring on through fear or disdain.

Mila: Arresting the vicious cycle

People test whether they deserve to be saved, whether they're worth it. While they can't allow themselves to feel they're worthy of life, or even that they want life, they want other people to want them to live. I guess that's easier than finding a part of you that doesn't hate you. It's less breathtakingly presumptuous than daring to entertain even the thought that I deserve to live and then finding out that no one else thinks so, and may even prefer you not to be alive.

People desperately want to be loved. They don't think anybody ever has or ever will love me, and I don't deserve it anyway. But I crave it. So as soon as *anyone* even suggests they like me or cares about me (even a slight friendship or acquaintance is enough), I react with wonder. If I have nothing else, someone's 'I care' overture sets up an 'I can't believe it' reaction. It's so amazing, it can't be true. So I test the care: 'Do they care enough to call me back?' 'Do they care enough to call a doctor?' 'Will they put up with this or that behaviour?' Now they don't seem to care about me as much, which just proves I'm not worth it. But I still want them to care, so I'll let them know by testing them even more.

This inevitable confusion over the concern and care produces testing behaviour, which leads to the 'carer' withdrawing somewhat. That fuels rejection and anger, and the 'testing' behaviours go on and on, getting more extreme, as 'carers' withdraw more and more, and people try even harder to regain the care and concern. The escalating behaviour is also fuelled by anger that the other doesn't love them, by effort to punish the other for not caring and by self-castigation for being so stupid as to think anyone would care about them. Eventually, they make the situation so extreme that someone is *forced* to 'care' for them.

Commentary from Duncan

Mila's perspective on the complexity of maintaining a relationship with someone who feels worthless at their core is revealing and emphasizes the need for adherence to the principles in Part Two of this book. If a clinician becomes embroiled in the cycle described above, it can only result in an unpleasant experience for the treating team. More importantly, it leads to a further experience of rejection for the person and supplementary evidence of their worthlessness and sense of being wrong. The principles of honesty and holding the line are paramount here. The type of behaviour that Mila describes is most likely to occur in the early stages of an encounter with a mental health team. The team therefore needs to provide an honest message of 'We are interested in understanding why you are doing this, but we'll not respond directly to it.' Team members then need to seek to engage the person in understanding why they are behaving as they do. The above message may need to be repeated consistently and often by numerous members of the team as the person seeks to test the level of care their team will offer.

Mila: Own the problem, accept the reality

Many people with BPD present with addictions. Cutting/burning/overdosing/purging (self-induced vomiting) can be as addictive as drugs or alcohol. In my experience, the pattern of addiction goes something like this: 'The more I do this (addictive) behaviour, and the more people I know who do it, the more I do it. I've got to know about this behaviour from people on my ward in the hospital and from cutting/overdosing/anorexia and suchlike websites.

Websites are particularly attractive because they give me a whole community and new ideas and advice, and they make it all seem so *normal*; in fact, they make my behaviour seem mild and in control, given how much people exaggerate online. Well, I've tried to stop doing this behaviour, but I've never managed. And because I've never overcome an addiction, it and other things that might help me are not really worth trying anymore. I despair of ever stopping voluntarily. And, besides, because there are other things I have so little control over, what's the point of trying anything anyway? And if that's the case, I don't even want to talk about those things anymore.

Essentially, the behaviour ends up being something separate from the motivations it originated from; it becomes an entrenched habit that serves different purposes for the people that are hurting—a crutch, a distraction, an escape, self-punishment. These types of destructive behaviours have to stop in the same way as any addiction, I suppose, but therapists have to be careful because focusing on the behaviour tends to escalate the impulse to indulge. People have to commit to stopping as a condition of treatment. We need to remember that for people with an addiction, stopping changes everything in their daily life. Every minute of every day they want to do it. And they can't—day after day. And, no, in my experience, it doesn't get easier with time. The desire eats at people until they want to scream. And so they return to the behaviour. Immediately, they're back where they were, and then some. The easiest time to quit is the first time they try. By the time they 'quit' for the nth time, everybody doubts them, including them.

I think the only way through with addiction is to have people admit the behaviour and explicitly state the motivation to stop. They need to tacitly, authentically state their intention not to do the behaviour. As part of this work, they also have to authentically commit to therapy, a good measure of which may focus on acceptance. They might need, for example, to accept that there's only so much drugs they can do, and that legal drugs don't make them happy. Legal drugs actually make people sleepy, so it's easier to ignore stuff. I suspect experience antidepressants rarely work for people with BPD/PTSD. The person might eventually also need to accept that they may never fulfil the motivation to quit for the duration of their lives, but that they can keep trying. Some patients also need support to accept that very likely others do not particularly like them, let alone love them. This simply has to be accepted.

Commentary from Duncan

Mila's words make us think of the times in our lives when we've been particularly upset, agitated or stressed. We know the physical states involved in these emotions are genuinely unpleasant, as they have to be, of course. If negative emotions weren't aversive, we wouldn't pay attention to things that are important, and we'd walk into the jaws of the sabre tooth tiger we always talk about when educating people about anxiety. People with borderline personality face a grim, and ultimately futile, struggle between trying to escape affect they not only fear but also find genuinely painful; they're overwhelmed by it.

It's therefore entirely understandable that addiction and BPD (and trauma for that matter) go hand in hand. Any addictive or compulsive behaviour is effective in moving a person, and often also the people attempting to treat them, away from the underlying feelings, memories and encounters that the person is invested in avoiding. We can quite understand how a victim of incest and its concomitant shame would find solace in a community of 'like-minded' adults, swopping information on self-harm, restricting food or tips on vomiting after eating. It's the immersion in these behaviours that keeps the person away from the source of the problem.

This issue is one directly addressed in dialectical behaviour therapy which asks people to commit to stopping their maladaptive attempts to cope with distress. This type of therapy feels harsh at times, akin to saying to someone, 'You have to stop using these ways of coping *before* I teach you any better ways of coping.' But it's also entirely necessary, as the effort required to complete mindfulness exercises twice a day requires much more commitment than smoking a joint or the simple fantasy that the pain will end through suicide. Without this clearly stated and genuinely intended commitment to change in place, we consider that treatment will always fail. Such is the task at hand if people are to begin to alter how they fundamentally approach their reality—their personality, in other words.

Mila: Self-harm as self-identity

For me, self-harm began by cutting started as a secret, a punishment and a flirtation with suicide, when I was about 12. I kept it to myself until I was 15, when someone I knew saw the marks. It was only after that that it became a manipulator for me. For a few years, it was a secret escape, but once someone knew and reacted, it became much more of a split reaction: part of it was escape, part of it was to feel in control, part of it was to feel cared for, and part of it was, well, because after I while couldn't stop myself.

It's kind of the same with the eating disorder behaviour. It starts as a secret but eventually becomes known. And the trouble is that it becomes so persuasive and so strong it takes over your life. Thinking or talking about it, even tangentially, always makes it worse. It's like one of those knots where any movement at all just pulls it tighter.

I think, too, that cutting or purging becomes part of your identity. It's extremely hard to be known as a cutter or anorexic and then to renounce the behaviour. People assume that if they can no longer see a symptom, then the problem is resolved and you're 'better' or 'over it', when all you hear is 'failure' and 'fat'. You're still miserable—in fact, even more so, because now you are both fat and unhappy. But people can't 'see' the pain anymore. One of the most painful things a person has ever said to me was, 'Oh you've put on so much weight! You must be so much happier now, not looking like a freak all the time.' That sparked six months of restriction and purging and a weight loss of 20 kilograms.

Commentary from Duncan

It's reasonably easy to discuss with a person how they might be using self-harm as a maladaptive way of regulating their emotion. People commonly report the physical pain they feel or the image of the blood flowing from their skin as a welcome distraction from their emotional pain. It is not so easy to discuss with someone how they might be using similar self-harm or other self-destructive behaviour as a way of seeking attachment or as an effort to recruit a caring response in others.

I remember being eight years old and struggling to complete my maths lesson at school. A previous teacher had made me the laughing stock of the class a few years earlier for misunderstanding something, and I was deeply upset at the idea of getting this so wrong. Even now, I can remember my tears blurring the pencil marks on the text book, the lines swimming before my eyes. My teacher asked me what was wrong, and instead of saying I couldn't do it, something I assume I thought was shameful, I lied and said I felt ill.

My mum dutifully picked me up and regarded my sceptically. She took me to the doctor and sat quietly when he inevitably said he couldn't see anything wrong with me. I was allowed to stay at home but felt uneasy, as I clearly hadn't been believed. When I tried this again a few weeks later, my mother firmly told me to stop pretending to be ill and sent me straight back to school, no doubt telling my teacher I had been faking.

That evening, she sat me down and coaxed me into admitting I was struggling with math, something that felt like a major admission at the time. She helped me with it, thereby teaching me not to bullshit her and that there wasn't anything shameful about asking for help with school work. I wonder what would have happened if my mum had let me off school every time I felt sick. What if she had pursued the medical profession to find the mysterious thing that was wrong with me as opposed to trusting her instinct as a mother—challenging me and helping me with the real problem?

This is something I think about when, as a team, we are confronted by someone who persistently takes non-lethal overdoses, phones constantly or consistently self-harms. It seems some of these people are like me as an eight year old. They feel like, if they say what the real problem is, they will be rejected so they use a problem people have to respond to. It emphasises to me that if I respond to a person's efforts to mask the real problem I will not only encourage them to keep doing it more and, worse still, cause them to bury it deeper within themselves. Conversely, the only way I'm going to stand a chance of getting to the underlying problem is to not respond to the behaviour that masks the real problem and show I'm interested and willing to really know what is happening.

The people I work with are not eight and I am not their mother so, quite often, it isn't possible to talk about what is really happening underneath. In such a situation this approach at least gives me the sense I didn't make things too much worse.

Mila: The value of meds

The biggest fear I have is of a doctor taking away the meds I need. I've found that doctors always want to go down not up on meds, so if I agree to reduce or stop, they probably won't allow me to increase or restart. Basic principle: If I ask for a particular drug, I'll not be given it. Having a doctor who did the opposite—who gave out and increased my meds all the time—actually let me relax about them being taken away. It also allowed me to realize that drugs can only do so much, and usually all they seem to do is sedate me. Which is nice, but it keeps me in a holding pattern that's not optimal for therapy.

I think that a lot of people who've been on meds for years are curious about what it would be like without them. But they are reluctant to experiment in case someone says, 'You did without the meds for a week, therefore you don't need them.' Having a stash reduces anxiety. The meds are there if you need them, so it makes it easier to stick it out without them. Without a stash, the person tends to panic about what to do when matters become overwhelming.

I did wonder aloud to Duncan about whether the medical team could come up with an alternative 'last resort', something as a substitute for suicide/self-harm/overdosing, etcetera. An 'off' switch—like something to knock you out for 48 hours. But then Duncan said it was just another way of avoiding reality. Which is true, I suppose. Still it would be (1) less harmful than other behaviours, and (2) an ambulance at the top of the cliff. But I do see his point. It's tricky. Unconsciousness is still the holy grail of meds, to me.

Commentary from Duncan

I never ceased to be amazed to witness the transformation that occurs in people when they are confronted by a psychiatrist. Mila firstly attests to the way in which people are afraid of the power their psychiatrist has to take away the medication they feel reliant on. In addition, people have often suggested they fear that since the psychiatrist has the power to section them they must manage the impression they give, entering the kind of cagey cat and mouse game described above. Even the most skilled, empathic and compassionate psychiatrist must understand the effect they can have on people simply because of their job title and understand how much harder they will have to work to build a genuinely collaborative relationship with someone as a result. Only then can the dance end and more honest conversations start.

Secondly, Mila describes the way in which she uses medication. She changes dosages herself and keeps a 'stash' to reassure herself if she might need it. I suspect these examples of 'poor compliance' are commonplace. So, again, a prescriber will have to work hard to build the type of relationship where someone is able to be honest about *how* they're using their medication and, more importantly, why they have taken their own approach.

Prescribing clinicians and teams can become understandably nervous, and sometimes somewhat sanctimonious, when someone uses their medication in an unorthodox fashion. This is entirely justified. Should an adverse event occur, prescribers will be held to account for their practice, and that account will include their efforts to educate the person on the importance of following the prescribed approach. That said, we know from health behaviour research that the level of compliance with any prescribed medication is often surprisingly poor. I'm sure I'm not alone in failing to complete a course of antibiotics or having a reserve of unused prescription pain killers in the medicine chest—'just in case'. The principle of honesty is key here in moving outside of a person's perception that the psychiatrist is the guardian of some medicalized 'solution' and towards a more frank conversation about how the use of medication (as well as its limitations) fits with what other changes a person needs to make if their experiences are going to begin to change for the better.

Mila's proposition that she would benefit from a temporary, drug-induced oblivion also raises interesting questions about the role of medication. I do not think this is a good idea, as she herself explains. Instead, for me, it raises the important question of whether, through trying to help, we inadvertently assist someone to learn to rely on an external medium to avoid experiences. If someone feels worthless because they were treated as nothing when they were a child, this feeling of worthlessness provides the bearing back to experiences that didn't so much reflect worthlessness but the painful reality of an abusive, dysfunctional parent. Someone may lack the skills or motivation to undertake this kind of work. That is fine if they are making an informed decision not to. They may accordingly choose medication as a way of avoiding reminders of the past. I think we need to be cautious about reassuring someone with BPD that the drugs they are prescribed will be, in themselves, a direct route to wellness.

Jade: No one has to do it alone

The nurse is looking at me, but talking to my husband: 'So she thinks she has a tracker in her stomach?'

'I do,' I quickly interrupt.

She looks and me and smiles. It's clear she thinks I'm crazy. They all do. I don't really care what they think, although I'm sure it was only because they don't know any better, and I comfort myself with that fact.

This was my life shortly after the birth of my third son, living in an alter-reality. Yes, that's right, I'm a mother to three boys. I was diagnosed with mental illness when I was 16, although the problems started a lot earlier than that. After the birth of my son, the anxiety that had kept me awake before his birth began really taking over and causing physical problems. And then the words of my best friend began ringing in my ears. She chose to end her own life. She'd told me it would be too selfish for her to have kids because how, she asked me, could she be a good mother with a mental illness? The risk of passing her illness on to her kids would be selfish, too. I questioned myself. I questioned everything. What she'd said to me haunted me for a long time: 'How can you be a good mother when you have a mental illness?' \

So I stopped. I stopped being a good mother. I didn't want to be alive. I wanted to take myself away from my children. I turned away from them. I turned away from myself.

Every time I went into hospital, it was a relief. I didn't have to be the mother I didn't want to be. It would all be easier, better, if I didn't have children. That's what I thought. That's what I believed. None of this was because I didn't love them. I love them fiercely. I love them deeply. This was all because I did love them. If I couldn't be a good mother because of having a mental illness, they deserved much, much better than me.

So things were bad, very bad. And for what seemed like a very long time, things were the same for me, in and out of hospital and heavy doses of medication: this was my life. But one day, after a series of events, I realized I had to change or I was going to lose my family, the family I had so badly wanted, the family I loved, or they were going to lose me. Yes, things were hard, very hard, but they needed to change. I had three little boys who needed their mum in their lives.

On speaking with my doctor after I'd been in respite yet again, we decided that we'd cut back my medication and there would be no more hospital admissions. I was happy with the decision at first, but after a while things got hard again, and I was scared about the decision we'd made. I was frightened that if things didn't work out, the kids would be left without a mother altogether, and my husband without a wife.

The mental health team put extra support in place through the means of Pathways, and with the support of everybody, things slowly started to change. It wasn't an easy journey, but having the backing of the doctor and knowing that things had to change before I self-destructed was a real motivation for me. When I was on so much medication, I was constantly drowsy and felt nothingness. Being off so much medication gave me a clearer head, so I was able to be in charge of my own recovery.

I learned that change is a hard thing because I couldn't change the fact I have a mental illness. I couldn't change the fact that the world around me could sometimes be so cruel. But I could change my outlook—I could learn how to live with this debilitating illness.

It took a while, but I re-learned how to look after my children. One day, I was sitting with my eldest son, and he said something funny. And I laughed! I actually laughed. Might not seem like much, but that feeling of laughter felt like the best feeling in the world. After almost a year and a half of darkness, there was finally that glimpse of hope, that of a mother enjoying spending a moment with her child. It was at that point, I realized you can be a good mother and live with mental illness.

I used to wonder how I could be a good parent if I had a mental illness. Now I know how I can be: laughing with them, loving them like I've never loved anybody, trying. You get points for trying—ha, ha. And making mistakes; every parent does, mental illness or not.

But, ultimately, it's been a matter of accepting myself and understanding my illness. And teaching my children it is okay to ask for help—always. No-one has to do it alone.

Commentary from John

More than anything else, Jade's account reveals the benefits of taking an honest approach with a person. Having the courage to name what her fears may have been in terms of her family life and the impact of her fears on her marriage meant a different approach could be taken. Jade's unusual perceptual experiences and the gamut of medicalized treatment that followed became a welcome distraction from the intolerable stress of home life. Jade's description reveals how she herself realized she had to take steps to change things and, through the willingness of the team to listen to her story and respond to her accordingly, she was able to collaborate with us in removing the obstacles that had maintained her avoidance of home life.

Mara: The place of trust

Wow, who knew I could feel this free, this alive, this much at peace. Certainly not me in the beginning, in fact not even till the end of therapy.

Three years ago, I was at the bottom of a very dark pit, felt unworthy of life itself, that this was all my fault and I deserved what had happened to me. The idea of being able to heal was not even a reality. I thought maybe I could fake it, get a band-aid to cover up the mess that was my life (and that it would take about six weeks to do it). Yeah, right!

Acknowledging that I had a problem, that I wasn't coping was the first step I think. This was totally new to me, the feelings of not being in control, well maybe not that new, really, as I soon discovered. It was how I felt when I was a child, and going back to those feelings was so scary.

The problem with therapy and accepting help is in trusting someone else when all you have learned is not trust. How could they expect me to expose myself, because that's what it felt like they were asking me to do? Hell, if I'd hidden it for 40 years or so from even myself, they surely couldn't want me to actually say these words out loud; I couldn't even say them in my head.

Talking was really hard. I'm very good at distracting, changing and going off topic, and Kate allowed me to do this, but she'd subtly bring me back to what was really happening for me. Actually, Duncan would do this too—let me have my distraction, then bring me back again, to the task at hand.

It felt so uncomfortable, and I couldn't understand why she would even want to bother. I was sure there were other people more in need of them than I was. But through weekly sessions, and sometimes more often if needed, I learned to feel valued as a person in my own right, not just because of my past. I began to build that trust, really slowly, and I don't think I was even aware of it at the time, but it was there.

Being accepted for who I was in my darkest moment, not being judged for thoughts that scared me, was so helpful. It meant I could talk out loud my thoughts of self-harm and suicide, and get honest feedback. It meant I knew I'd not be criticized for them but have acknowledged that feeling this way was okay, but also having suggested to me that there are other options.

Kate taught me mindfulness amongst other things; well, actually, she taught me that I was a person and how to be a person. Seems big, and it is really. I didn't understand the scattered, irrational person I had become; this wasn't me. How could I go from travelling the world to hardly being able to make it to my letterbox? Getting an understanding of what PTSD meant and understanding the symptoms, where they came from and why they were happening, really helped me. I could put at least the rational side of my mind to work on something.

The hardest part was getting the emotional side to work alongside this, finding the 'wise mind' in this. I understood emotions from a rational standpoint, but I didn't understand how they worked in me. Can't have a 'wise mind' if you don't have access to half of it.

It was also a stumbling block with the EMDR[2] as well, as I couldn't understand what it was I was feeling, physically and emotionally; and really I was quite comfortable with not feeling. I thought it had worked for me so far, so we could just keep on going this way. The problem was I was feeling this stuff and not understanding it, or how to react or accept it. The paperwork on defining and understanding emotions was just brilliant; I could rationally understand the words and know what they meant, and could in turn place those feelings and body sensations inside me. I had words and an understanding of what I was feeling, I could actually allow this to happen and not react irrationally. I understood that it was normal and even okay

Having support when going to ACC[3] appointments was huge, too; having someone on my side that was looking out for my interests when I couldn't—someone who would even open the letters for me when I was too scared.

When EMDR with Duncan was suggested, I went along with it (again with this notion that it would take six weeks). I trusted Kate and, to a lesser extent John, so I went on their faith that this was the right thing to do—after all my decisions over the last year or so hadn't exactly been helpful. Those first few sessions were not eagerly anticipated to say the least (well I'm not sure I ever eagerly anticipated it). This meant I was going to have to come face to face with my demons. I thought I was going to have to jump right into it, but thankfully that wasn't the case.

I remember in those first sessions doing a timetable of my early life—and managing to avoid all talk of abuse. Thought I had done quite well really. It was a good way to break the ice, to get to know Duncan, how he talked and moved. He appeared calm, had an even tone, and he became a person in his own right, with a life. Him talking about himself helped with this, helped build a relationship, helped build up that trust. This was important.

If I was going to have to share this really important stuff, then I needed to know how this other person was going to react, if I could trust them with my deepest, darkest and most personal moments. I also got to realize that it just wasn't the sexual abuse that I was dealing with, but with attachment and abuse from my mother, and the shame that was ingrained in my personality. Working with some of those memories first helped me get a handle on the EMDR stuff and how Duncan worked and acted as a person. Of course, then came the hard part.

When sharing stuff, I would watch for any sign that Kate or Duncan was disgusted by me, by what I was saying. I looked for subtle movements in body language, change in voice over and over and over again. I didn't see any, and this was just as scary: What could this mean? Duncan would encourage me to use words, which was a challenge; well, it was more than a challenge really; bloody impossible. Sometimes he'd put the words out there for me which helped—made them available, and I could use them again if I chose to. It wasn't just all coming from me. Words have so much power, which I came to realize along this journey. Even being able to say the name of my cousin was overwhelming. But having control over words, be they about a memory or a name, meant that I, not the memory, was in control. It kinda put the scary, shameful feelings to the side.

Creating the fairy circle was really important. I could access the scared child part of me, the angry teenager, the wanderlust adult, the teacher, and me now. I could build up a

---

[2] Eye movement desensitization and reprocessing therapy.

[3] Accident Compensation Corporation, a government-based organisation that provides no-fault personal injury cover, including mental injury such as post-rape mental trauma.

relationship with myself; see things from a different perspective, get to understand how all this stuff affected the various parts of me. I could even share and give compassion to all those different parts of me. Connecting all those parts helped in the overall integration process and we found other pieces too—the fog that would settle if emotions became too confusing, the big stick that was my mother's voice of irrationality, but in the end became my safeguard. I have now come to appreciate the strength that I had as a child and teenager; not judge them for their actions and reactions but really understand them—well, me really.

The memory work was just so overwhelming at times. The memories were in bits and pieces, seemed to have a life of their own and could force their way into the present so forcefully that I often got confused as to what was then and what was now. For the child, the memory hadn't ended, was still happening, even to the point where I could physically still feel it. Pulling together the fragments of a memory, all the sharp spiky bits and create a smooth complete memory, with a beginning and an end, was very important to the child. Being able to create a story around it meant I was able to file it away in its place, along with other memories of my childhood. They will always be there, part of me, but they don't own me anymore. I own them.

Going into different memories meant being totally emerged in them sometimes, and finding a way back to reality was hard, really, really hard. I could feel so consumed by it. Holding the metal sphere helped with grounding, as did the volley-bird and doing the 5 4 3 2 1 game. It took so much brainpower sometimes to find words to describe a simple object, but it got to the point that I could use this on my own. Bringing in my teddy was a great idea. I had something I could hold onto that was linked to part of me, to a nice part of me. When it came to feelings and emotions, I needed a hug sometimes, and hugging this bear gave me comfort, release and even permission to feel.

The moment when I realized it wasn't my fault was so huge, I just can't really explain it. Putting that memory into perspective, seeing it for what it really was—my cousin taking advantage of a child's need for love. I could find compassion for that child, which I never had before. And the teenager could direct the anger where it should have been directed— towards him not her. It wasn't my fault. It *isn't* my fault!

But the best was yet to come—freedom and peace. I never in anytime during this process understand that this would happen, that it could happen, that it was even a remote possibility. This list of memories that I had to work through just evaporated, and they became, well, just memories. Yes, Duncan said this would happen, and it wasn't that I didn't believe him. I just couldn't see how this was going to happen. Still I went on his faith, and I'm so glad I did.

This peace I feel now is brilliant—unimaginable really. The fairy circle isn't as important anymore because it's all part of me. All the parts of me are integrated together, the good stuff and the bad stuff. The therapy has shaped who I am now, and through this process I don't have to hide parts of me away in shame and pretend they don't exist.

I could paint this rosy picture, say that there were not setbacks or pitfalls, that I didn't feel worse at times, because I can't because I did. But I got to a point where I knew help was there; not that I necessarily always asked for it, but it was there. If I couldn't understand what I was feeling then, they would help me work it out. Understanding body sensations, and the thoughts running through my head, what this meant for me now and what it had meant for me in the past. Having people that cared, cared if I lived or died when even I didn't.

But, most important, I think, was letting me guide the process, letting me feel as if I was in control, nudging me in the right direction—be that towards stopping the EMDR if I felt that was needed, respite, medication, other ways of handling situations, or even just coffee.

I am a whole and complete person now. Well, not finished complete and together complete, but with new things to discover, with a strong sense of who I am, what I feel and my impact on the world around me.

Commentary from Duncan

It's difficult to distil Mara's three-year interaction with our team into a few short conclusions. When I read her account, I'm struck by how important the human factors in our encounter were to her. While writing this, I'm also thinking about my next appointment in 30 minutes' time. Most of the thoughts are about technique. What can I do to move this person towards better emotional understanding and therefore acceptance? What will edge her towards addressing the traumatic experiences that led her to use hostility as a means of defending herself? Reading Mara's account makes me think more about how this woman I'm about to see will perceive me as a person and how I can best behave given they have such mistrust of other people and expect to be rejected or abandoned at any time.

I also think Mara's account gives great hope. Not only was she on the brink, but she had spent her whole life running from the memories that not only haunted her but shaped her 'borderline' personality. By encouraging her to take responsibility for her own life and by making an active effort to listen to and reflect back her story, we helped her understand, rationally at least, the nature of her predicament. From that point, the hard work could start—mining her past for evidence contrary to the deeply held negative beliefs she had about herself. Mara's comments demonstrate that forming new paradigms is difficult, confronting but ultimately possible. She espouses the rewards therein better than I ever could.

John: Sometimes it just goes beautifully, and what it privilege it is to be there

Veronica is the ideal patient, bright, articulate and able to join the dots. One of the best things about writing book is that it made us look carefully at what we do. We've just completed the first draft of the chapter on diagnosis, and that work has confronted us with how the initial presentation can so easily and effectively cloud subsequent interactions, particularly when we're busy.

I nonetheless take Veronica's family history of bipolar into account as she describes poor sleep, irritability, high libido and overspending. Furthermore, she's just bought a business! But there is also something about Veronica and her story. Growing up and feeling lonely until her early teens, she became aware of how men noticed her attractiveness. She had a number of brief relationships and, when they were commented on, she acknowledged that the men she dated were physically similar to her father. She describes her father as a 'bad boy' who flirted with barmaids and had mistresses. Although he was never inappropriate with Veronica, her mother accused Veronica of being 'a tart'. Veronica agrees that her mother may have resented their close relationship. Given that her brother's bipolar disorder was not as clear as initially described, he seems to me more like a young man rebelling than a man with an episodic mood disorder. Also, given Veronica's similar lack of a clear, episodic history, I wonder if there could be another way of understanding her difficulties. When I ask her when she'd next like to see me, she says, tomorrow, next week: 'I want to understand myself,' she explains.

Veronica returns one week later. Our conversation has stirred up some ghosts, as she puts it. We begin to talk about her dad dying and how hard that was for her when he was so important in her life and when all around her was so hurtful. The following week, she says she feels awful, sad and wants to die. She's frightened she'll be hospitalised and therefore wants medication. We decide on lamotrogine 25mg, although I let her know I'd prefer not to prescribe anything. I think Veronica is very likely able to make use of psychotherapy: from the beginning of our talks together, she's been able to make links with her mood and the loss of her dad, the loss of her boyfriends and the way she's used sexual attractiveness to survive loneliness and sadness.

Next time she says me, she says she's slept for the first time: 'It's the tablets.' I'm a bit surprised and a bit hurt, and as gently as I can I suggest she's sleeping because she's talking and managing unfamiliar feelings. Veronica still thinks it's the medication, but she continues to explore her relationships with other men and her feelings. She tells me about a book she's found called *Fearful of Feeling*. It led her to remember pleading when she was a child with her mother to stop drinking. Her mother, she concludes, has always preferred alcohol and her increasingly younger boyfriends over her daughter. However, her mother noticed when she became truant, sexually aware and began mixing with the 'naughty girls' (to again use her words). As a result, she was sent to boarding school.

Veronica's way of coping, acting out rather than experiencing, talking and understanding, has persisted for a long time, but now Veronica is beginning to see how it might all link together. A new sadness rolls in but without the earlier desperation. She also begins to recognize that she developed another way of coping in adulthood—eagerness to please. Frightened of being alone again, she does the bidding of her partner. Nothing violent, but just subsumed by him and his needs.

One day, she tells me, her mother arrived at her and her partner's home, wanting to stay. Veronica tried to please her, spending what little money she'd managed to save to improve the house. Her mother, however, sat on the newly cleaned sofa, feet on the newly cleaned carpet and drank. Veronica can now see what she was doing at the time—trying to appease her mother, but she's still taken aback when I wonder whether she'd like to kill her mother.

The following week, Veronica arrives at her session. 'I've killed my mother,' she announces, but then adds, with a smile, 'Only metaphorically! And it felt good.' I ask her where she feels that in her body. She pauses before she speaks and then straightening her body says, 'In my back.' Another pause, followed by a delighted 'I've got a backbone!'

At our next session, Veronica tells me I've unleashed beasts. I haven't. Rather, Veronica's begun to trust her feelings and to act from these rather from loneliness and eagerness. As we finish our work, Veronica reflects, 'I've been part of a roller coaster all my life. There's never been a straight piece of road. Whenever there was, I've rocked and shook it up with my stupid choices.' Empty, bereft for what she's lost but with the calm and understanding of what had happened and now knowing who she is, she says she isn't and *wasn't* mentally ill.

Veronica: Losing reliance on labels

Finding yourself sitting in a chair in psychiatrist's office comes as a shock. It did to me anyway. I couldn't figure out how I'd got there. How had this happened to me? I knew that I'd got to a point in my life when I felt completely alone, when I'd upset just about everyone around me, where I was only just coping, getting through each day in a manic muddle, and that I needed help. I felt that I could barely function, and knew that I needed help, and fast. I was either in the depths of despair or in a state of ecstatic bliss, and it wasn't sustainable.

I'd read about bipolar disorder and, self-diagnosed, took myself off to tell my GP. He agreed with me, which was a relief. Being able to put a name to my muddle meant that I finally had an answer to my increasingly self-destructive behaviour. A few pills and everything would be back to normal. Problem solved. Great!

But I'd landed in the office of Dr John Little, and even though I told him many times that I was bipolar and that he *had* to give me some drugs pronto, he was reluctant from the second session onwards. Instead, he asked me questions, got me thinking, got me remembering. He did give me some drugs, but at an extremely low dosage. They were more of a psychological crutch than answering a chemical need. I slept better, though, and that made a big difference.

Looking back at a childhood I'd buried, and recognizing how traumas that I'd experienced in my past were affecting my life was a painful, difficult process. Talking to Dr Little helped. Writing helped. I read, too, anything I could about the healing process after trauma and mental illness. Through talk therapy with Dr Little, I recognized the destructive influence that two abusive people were continuing to have in my life, and I was able to put up the necessary boundaries to keep these people at bay. It's important to recognize when outside forces are at work, and also when our behavioural patterns need to be owned. It has taken a lot of self-evaluation and thinking for me to get to a point where I can see so much of what has gone wrong in my life is not a part of a mental illness, but about circumstances and mistakes and dealing with other people's addictions. Writing helps me see clearly, as does meditation. Writing helps me to see clearly, to see things for what they are.

When I first walked into Dr Little's office, I had no ability to see clearly. I couldn't get separate my self-loathing from my loathing of others. It took time and work to put the jumble in my head into any sort of order. I was terrified to make friends, I knew losing them hurt too much, and I was in no fit state for any kind of relationship. Today, my circle of friends is growing. I am back at university doing a Master's degree, and I live in my own skin very happily. I maintain clear boundaries with my ex and my mother, as hard as that is at times, and I am healthier than I was skin very happily. I can't recommend meditation enough, either, for bringing that initial order and peace to a busy mind.

When Dr Little wouldn't diagnose me as bipolar, I was angry, and for a good while too. I'd clung to that label as a solution as a drowning woman might a piece of driftwood. But now I'm incredibly grateful. I'm no longer on medication, and I continue to go from strength to strength. Turns out my problems were not chemical; they were all external. Talk therapy brought them to the fore, allowed me to explore their continuing influence and to deal with them. Therapy has been an invaluable experience. It has completely changed my life.

Commentary from John

Veronica narrowly avoided a diagnosis of bipolar affective disorder (Type II) and its attendant treatments. Overspending is such a problem with bipolar affective disorder that it and the buying of the business formed an important part of the early diagnostic criteria. However, when I asked her about buying the business, her reply was simple: 'I made a bad decision.' The avoidance of the wrong diagnosis also came about because Veronica was so receptive to the possibility that other influences in her life may've been more instructive than she previously contemplated. Critically, she could also begin to feel. She spent the time between sessions trying to understand and make the connections in her life story and how they shaped the concerns that led her to see us in the first instance. Those abilities helped us help her heal.

From the Team

In one of my first training sessions as a trainee psychologist, my teacher told a story about a man who arrived at their forensic mental health unit one morning who was beside himself with rage and wanted to hurt someone. The team deliberated about how they were going to deal with this situation and decided they would *all* calmly approach him and convey the same message. So all 11 staff members left the sanctuary of the office and stood shoulder to shoulder and approached the man. When he tried to single out the people he was particularly angry with, their colleagues would simply restate the message to him. He soon left.

The two of us find we're often overwhelmed by the demands of working with people with BPD. It's therefore been interesting talking to our team about this book. For us, the comments from the administrative members of the team especially have been especially valuable. The stories and reflections from members of the team that follow include a couple of our own.

Heather: The value of boundaries

The administrative team at Kapiti Mental Health has 51 years of mental health administration experience between the three of them. With that much experience, there is a lot of knowledge, and we've also witnessed many changes within that time.

Sometimes a 'day at the office' can be one crisis after another; other times much calmer and more planned. The professionalism, decision-making and skill of the clinician has a huge impact on how things are managed on a daily basis.

One of the things we've noticed over this time is that the clinicians are more open to input from Admin; today, they take on board our observations of clients in the waiting-room. There are often times when people behave quite differently towards us than they do when they are with the clinician. They can be demanding and aggressive with us but then become immediately quiet and charming when the doctor arrives, or they may be absolutely calm in the waiting-room but start to cry or become more agitated when they see the clinician.

Sometimes we notice a person who is acting as if they are being followed, constantly looking out the door to the car park or sitting curled up into a corner of the couch. We can pass on these observations to a clinician who is unaware of these behaviours.

Another noticeable difference over the years has been the setting of clear boundaries between clinician and client. For example, a clinician will tell us that he or she won't take any phone calls from the client, but the client is welcome to leave a message. The boundary tells the client that the clinician won't be constantly available to them. But the client also know there are set appointments in place during which they will have 100 percent of the clinician's attention. There are times when clients call constantly, sometimes five, six or more times a day.

Admin has a multitude of other duties to perform, so we can get frustrated when more than one client calls in this frequently each day, or if the client is upset, insisting their situation is an emergency. Clear boundaries between clinicians and clients reduce a lot of the above behaviour, so making make a huge difference to Admin's workload. The specifics of the boundary for any one client made it easier for us to explain the clinician's request to them, and it meant we were no longer acting as 'gate-keepers' all the time.

After I returned to the clinic from a 12-month maternity-leave break, I found a noticeable difference in relation to some of the clients who'd previously taken up a lot of our administrative time with their numerous daily phone calls and urgent requests. For example, one client who'd been told they were only allowed to call on a Tuesday was accepting of this rule and appeared much calmer.

Sometimes we'll have a sobbing client on the phone, telling you they need help and *now* and sometimes they'll present at the desk demanding to be seen immediately (pleas and behaviour we may've heard and seen from the same client many times over). But sometimes there is something much more subtle within an interaction that alerts you this call or visit is different. Something about the client's voice, expressions, behaviour just doesn't sit right. It's almost like a sixth sense. The intuition may come from the experience you have of that client or from the relationship you've formed with them over many years. Having that knowledge and then deciding to talk to the clinician and explain your disquiet can make a real difference for both clinician and client. We know our clinicians really value our intuition.

Another marked difference I've noticed in recent years is the greater expectation that the client will be an active participant in decisions relating to medications, therapy and so on. The clinician is no longer the one who will necessarily dictate what needs to happen or happens, and they will not 'save' the patient again and again. Today, there is the expectation that the client will make a commitment to therapy in order that change happens.

Commentary from John and Duncan

Our administrator's account reminds us of Rosemary Draper's observation in Chapter 5 that successful outcomes (and unsuccessful ones) involve the entire way an organization relates to a particular patient. Heather's account highlights the importance of Admin's role in 'holding the line', something that is only possible given their humanity and the clear approach held by the entire team. It also emphasises how people modify their behaviour for the benefit of clinicians and therefore the invaluable nature of these observations from reception staff. You have to ask them, though! The account also provides an informal but gratifying suggestion that these approaches genuinely contain people, are therapeutic and can make mental health teams healthier environments in which to work.

Kate: The importance of formulation

'I can't get her to stay on track,' I fret one week. The video, which Duncan is also watching, shows Lou, who I've been working with in my capacity as a psychiatric nurse over several appointments, talking relentlessly. Barely pausing for breath, Lou describes difficulties in her work life and social life and with her family. I've tried to use an agenda to corral Lou into a meaningful conversation but so far without success.

More specifically, I've been trying to reduce Lou's distress, but she's doing her best to avoid her underlying distress by talking. Her transference was along the lines of 'If I avoid meaningful, emotional connection to my problem, you may not reject me,' reciprocated by my countertransference—that of boredom, annoyance and fantasizing about the end of the relationship, a pattern played out in Lou's life. Discussing my feelings about Lou with Duncan helps me gain understanding of what might be happening within my relationship with her.

One of Duncan's basic themes in supervision is the idea of being mindful of where, in the process, a therapist is following the basic guideline of assessment, formulation and treatment. Once Duncan and I start formulating the situation, we realize we don't have sufficient information about aspects of Lou's past, her experience of rejection and how she was treated by her caregivers when she was upset. I realize I've been attempting to alleviate distress without fully formulating the underlying problem.

During my next sessions with Lou, I manage to probe deeper into Lou's past and beliefs and so gain the information Duncan and I consider necessary. I come to understand why Lou developed her beliefs that she would be rejected when upset, that she was a failure and that she had always been different from other people. I put this formulation to Lou, highlighting the underlying mechanisms of the behaviour we'd been discussing at a much more superficial level for some months.

'How to lose a patient in one easy session,' I joke at my next supervision meeting with Duncan. Lou, understandably rattled by my change of direction, had essentially said, 'This is too confronting, too difficult. I'll just make my own way.' However, two weeks later, she returns, saying she does want to work on what I've identified. I know that the work from this point on is not necessarily going to be straightforward for either of us, and that its success is far from guaranteed. However, through a sound formulation, the work at least stands a chance of being successful. With Lou's problematic beliefs now clearly stated, both she and I have gained a clear mutual understanding of what our focus should be.

Commentary from Duncan

As I've have become more senior, I've been increasingly asked to provide supervision for people, such as Kate, who are learning and striving to improve their therapy skills. This is good; it's much easier than doing the therapy oneself! I always encourage supervisees to record as much of their work as possible, to watch themselves and me in supervision. It's time consuming, but there are fewer better ways to learn and spot bad habits.

The lesson at the heart of this experience with Lou for Kate was the role that formulation played in helping her overcome an encounter with a client who had taken her to the point of trying to find a reason to end their work. If that had occurred, it would have reinforced Lou's view of herself. I have long maintained that if the work doesn't focus on the underlying problem, there is a danger of doing more harm than good. The best encounters, obviously, are therapeutic for a client. Protracted, non-therapeutic encounters are almost always unhelpful and increase the risk of therapist burnout.

Kate: Remaining strong

'Hey Kate, I've met someone whom I think you'd work really well with.' My team leader had just conducted his initial assessment of Mara (who we met earlier), and is keen for me, as a community psychiatric nurse, to be involved in her therapy.

I arrange to meet Mara. She's presently in respite, her diagnosis post-traumatic stress syndrome, secondary to childhood sexual abuse. When I meet her, what strikes me the most is her fear and bewilderment. She stutters, struggling to articulate her agitation: 'I don't know what's happening to me. Why am I like this? I don't know what to do.' What I know is that I need to show her straight away that I'm confident I can help her. I'm relieved when she says she's willing to work with me.

And thus begins our journey together, the two of us sitting in a tiny damp room at Respite, our feet planted on the floor, noticing the support of the chairs we're sitting on, our hands on our knees in an upturned posture, both of us breathing together, following what will become an important mantra: 'In and out. Deep and calm. Slow and relaxed. Easy. Smile. Present moment, my moment.' I write this on the back of my business card along with 'If you read this and are considering taking your life, please call the following number. You are not alone.' I give the card to Mara to put in her purse. It represents my first connection with her. It also reinforces for her my expressed willingness to be with her at all times.

The importance of 'being with' Mara seems to me imperative to the success of our relationship. I cannot stress enough the sense of aloneness that goes hand in hand with mental ill-health. I need to be a person whom Mara can learn to trust in a world that, for her, is full of untrustworthy people. Why should she trust anyone when her innocence was taken from her at such a young age? She was left to survive into adulthood, all the while employing childhood- and early adolescent-based strategies to keep people at a distance or under her own control in order to protect herself.

The first few months of our journey are predominantly concerned with life versus death, with Mara's risk of trusting versus my risk of not being able to prevent her from ending her life. The situation is perilous for a while. Old teenage coping mechanisms of self-harm through cutting combine with desperate measures to end her mental torture. These include overdosing and driving to a local lookout point with the intention of jumping, and they're matters that pepper-pot our conversations as she weighs up her options: 'Do I stay or do I go?' 'Is this too hard?' These are not just her thoughts. They're mine as well.

Through the steady mentoring of our psychiatrist, John, and the support of our team, I overcome my anxiety over 'not being good enough' to prevent Mara from ending her life. I need to acknowledge that even though those of us who work in mental health are professionals, we can only do so much to protect people from themselves. Suicide is always an option that none of us is powerful enough to take away from people. At times, my own sense of my powerlessness angers me, and I have to learn to rely on my co-workers. The support of the team is paramount to the decision-making process. What good will come of committing Mara to a psychiatric hospital? Won't it just limit her power even further? Maybe it'll only serve to allay our own anxieties or reinforce a long-term prognosis of ongoing ill health. So many questions ... In the end, I have to accept the adage, do your best. No one answer can suit every person and every situation; decision-making has to be on an individual basis.

In time, Mara reaches a point where she agrees to start working with Duncan, who thankfully has the availability to include her. I'm relieved she has come this far. I truly believe in her ability to recover. Other people (health care workers, family, friends) are not always so sure. They ask if her troubles are too hard to deal with. Is change really possible? I remain firm in my resolve that the answer is yes.

My determination that Mara can recover is what keeps me going. I have to hold onto hope, carry the 'candle of life' for her during the tough times when she is tempted to let the candle burn out. At times, I adopt the approach that my job is to 'be annoying'—to keep on getting in the way of her decisions to end her life. I 'loan' her a stuffed toy so that she can 'ground' herself whenever she goes into respite. I tell her she can return the toy when she no longer needs it. I see the toy as fulfilling the same purpose as the business card; simply by looking at it will remind Mara that someone cares. She isn't alone. The business card becomes dog-eared, and the toy misshapen through being squashed and heavily worked.

Mara remains alive and, after two years, returns the toy to me: 'Pass it on to the next person who needs it.' She also confirms how aggravating I've been to her during all the time we've worked together. 'I kept hearing your voice in my head saying to call for help or just for a chat. God, you were annoying Kate!'

I smile back at her. 'Good!'

Commentary from Duncan

What helped Mara recover? First, there was her willingness to trust in the process, to give up the fight of trying to 'make it all go away' through either her own self-criticism or destructive actions.

Second was the fact our work together took place within the support of a cohesive, knowledgeable and trusting team. Each of us could remain strong for Mara because of the willingness of all of us on the team to admit to our own personal insecurities and clinical dilemmas without fear of judgement from others. After all, isn't that what we request of those with whom we work? We encourage people to admit to insecurities, share dilemmas and trust in the safety that comes through the non-judgemental stance of others. We need to encourage ourselves to do the same.

John: Keeping a steady hand

'You're my last hope; I've tried everything, nothing works; I'm not worth it. I keep wanting to cry, to harm myself, to harm others. I've never wanted to do that before.'

'I wonder who you might be angry with,' I venture.

It's been two months since I arrived at the clinic, and Rose's appointment with me and Kate is her first. From the moment we meet her, we are struck by her sadness. We come to learn how much she has lost.

Despite her grief, Rose begins this first meeting by joking that she needs a new head! Kate asks what a new head might do for her. 'I wouldn't have the nasty thoughts and devils,' she replies. She's able to add that she doesn't want to harm herself, as we talk about her grandchildren. I notice how her sense of humour and distraction shift her dysphoria (profound state of unease).

At age 14, Rose was raped, became pregnant and had a termination. She suffered two head injuries, for which she received compensation. Opinion among the neurologists and opticians who saw her at the time was divided as to whether she had complex partial seizures or whether her visual disturbances were of psychological origin. Different neuropsychological assessments over ensuring years yielded similarly conflicting results. In addition to coping with obstructive sleep apnoea, deep vein thrombosis following her hysterectomy, high cholesterol levels, Type II diabetes and hypothyroidism, Rose also lost her employment.

Not long before coming to our clinic, Rose had taken another overdose of paracetamol. 'If Sheryl hadn't stopped me, I'd be dead.' I'd been warned by looking back through her notes that Rose narrowly avoided hepatocellular necrosis (serious liver damage) as far back as 1998. Her most recent admission showed her transaminases peaking at 5521U/L, the normal range for these liver enzymes being up to 27U/L. Three years before coming to see us, Rose has been taking 60 paracetamol tablets per day for months.

But Rose continues looking at me for my reaction to her tearfulness. I don't respond in the expected way, instead remaining quiet. Rose tries again, not with force, but just to check if I've missed her initial request. I'm reminded as I sit quietly opposite Rose of when I acted similarly while talking with one of my supervisors. I'd been lamenting a personal hurt. Instead of the much anticipated and comfortable acknowledgement, nurture was replaced by a question, 'What did you do differently?' My supervisor correctly saw me teetering on the edge of self-pity and bought me back into real time. Abruptly, I stopped feeling sorry for myself. His question made me look at my situation differently.

I ask Rose a similar question: 'How have you been able to keep yourself alive?'

'I use wise-mind, self-soothing distraction, one foot at a time,' she replies.

And so begins her story. There is something impressive about Rose. She recognizes what helps, I think. All I have to do is keep a steady hand. Soon, both of us know what the next step should be, and we've reached this understanding without comment. A complicit understanding passes between us. We both know that we could engage in the familiar and practised dance, but instead we're now curious about learning a new, different dance routine.

For months after our first meeting, Rose continued taking 60 paracetamol a day. But today, three years on, when she meets with me, she hasn't taken one paracetamol in the last 10 months. As is often the case, once the work is done, there is a stability without relapse. Rose has also regained her driver's license, is part of the community choir, chairs a local group, has managed a relationship break-up and overturned the symptoms described in her original neuropsychological reports. She also has a job. She tells me she very keen to be part of our book in order to show what is possible—to show others who struggle that they can move beyond such sadness.

Commentary from John

Applying the principles within this book was poignant given the seriousness of Rose's medical complications and risk of suicide. If I was to be true to our principles, then I had to maintain the same approach that had helped other people. There were the occasional stumbles on the dance floor but what an outcome. Rose is today actively involved in the community and hasn't seen us for three years.

John: 'Sorry, I can't do it today'

I don't want to be at work today. The long-term relationships of two of our four children have just ended, making it the third one this year. Our youngest has left to live and work overseas. I usually know when I am struggling. I feel an urgent tremulousness, a feeling of literally being on the edge. My mind is no longer quiet. It's harrowed and I struggle to think, let alone write. I want to go home, to rest and to recover. Instead, I stay at work. Someone asks me to do something. I oblige and do what is asked of me. It would've been easier to walk away. I want to retire.

Something makes me think back to the end of the 1970s when a quiet and comfortable New Zealand was impaled by the Springbok Tour. Seemingly from nowhere, an unspoken dilemma erupted. New Zealand was confronted with an issue it could no longer avoid. 'Training should protect the community against police violence,' a professor of psychiatry was quoted as saying. I remember thinking at the time that, of everyone, a professor of psychiatry should understand that people in the front line are human before they are professional, but perhaps the professor too was being human. Years later, I had an interview with the same professor. I was applying for the psychiatry training programme. Today, I wonder what would've happened if I'd expressed my thoughts the time.

I hadn't been long on the training programme when a new consultant psychiatrist made a passing comment that stayed with me for many years: 'You don't seem to get angry. I wonder what that's about?' It took me a long time before I could even begin to reflect on his question. I continued to be nice, avoiding conflict, trying to understand people's dilemmas. I also had an experience in my private life that enabled me to get a sense of anger's appeal. The feeling was extraordinary—excitement followed by the joy of discharged tension, of hidden hurt and sadness out in the open. The person with whom I'd been fighting was taken aback and contemptuous

She was attractive, and it was 2 a.m. by the time we finished our session. I was on call in my first year of training and wanted to rescue her. I began to fantasise how I might respond to her pleas. I was stunned with how I felt. I was happily married and knew that it was wrong. Yet these were the feelings, not acted upon, but present nevertheless. I could barely wait for the start of the next day as I fled to the head of department, 'Oh,' she said, 'haven't you ever experienced an erotic countertransference before?'

I'd been having more than my usual quota of coffee and chocolate. The week had been difficult. I'd been speaking to a friend, confirming his availability to locum during my sabbatical. He told me that a patient had killed himself and that our colleague had been pilloried in the press. I don't know the details of the incident. It wasn't relevant. We both knew our colleague, a kind and thoughtful man. In the same week, a patient didn't want to see me: 'I don't like him. He's arrogant.' James had wanted a medical solution for his difficulties: 'You're the doctor!' My attempt at hiding my dislike was lost, and he correctly saw my dishonesty.

Commentary from John

A series of moments: on a good day, and despite my best intentions to follow the principles that we've described in this book, sometimes I just can't do it. This feeling recently spurred my colleague Michael Tartaglia and I to write a paper on hatred. [69] Michael was just starting practice, and I was nearing the end, planning retirement. In preparation for the article, I reread some earlier work that proved helpful. [70, 71]

Michael and I also discussed the fact that we'd noticed in ourselves and in our colleagues that 'sinking feeling' akin to having to swallow a bitter pill, when there is something the clinician doesn't want to do but is having to do it anyway. Then comes the tendency to daydream about being somewhere else, doing something else with someone else. Or there may be feelings of ennui and tiredness and an inclination to watch the clock as the session winds on. We noted how, having become exhausted and thus intolerant, we began to doubt, over-investigate or question whether we were suited to work in the health sector. Feelings of inadequacy, hopelessness and despair intervened.

For some of the people we see, this state of mind may translate into penance for doctors who're unable to accept that they may hate someone who is ill and seeking their privileged help. Heroic but futile attempts to rescue or control through the excessive use of medications, restrictions and hospitalisations may ensue. The clinician can no longer take risks, has lost objectivity and, as a result, is now the helpless prisoner of the clinical interaction. Unacknowledged, the patient is rejected and suffers indifference or pity and ultimately is ejected from the relationship either by referral, transfer or premature discharge from a protecting environment.

These observations appear in all clinical practice irrespective of specialty, the aspirations to heal all, know all and to love all, but it is psychiatric staff who are particularly prone to this unrealistic hope. Unlike our medical and surgical colleagues who have a range of physical interventions, mental health specifically utilizes the warmth and humanity of ourselves as the therapeutic tool. As John Maltsberger and Dan Buie wisely observe, 'We often predicate our professional self-respect on not being rejecting, punitive, sadistic, murderous and disgusted in patients. An able therapist cannot permit himself [herself] to behave according to such feelings, but neither can he [she] afford the illusion that he differs from other human beings.' [71, p.628]

To help requires a capacity for empathy; to stand momentarily in the other's shoes and experience their pain, using what we've learned as a guide as to how best to respond. The difficulty with this is that there is often a close resemblance between our own painful experiences and those of the person, a situation that constantly threatens this capacity.

In order to manage, the dominant defence is to accentuate differences: 'they' are the sick or mad or needy ones; 'we' are the sane, strong, helping ones. The work in this case may be structured, via rigid timetables, programmes and hierarchy, to support the distance between the therapeutic team and the people its members see. Conversly, the dominant defence is to deny differences, to stand so much in the other's shoes that team members identify with the person as victim. This scenario can see us overwhelmed by people's pain and despair. Realistic task definition, by making some success possible, increases the capacity for both parties to overcome this negativity and top tolerate inevitable disappointments. [72] Reflecting on such feelings, discussing them with others, supervisors especially, has the advantage of helping us learn more about who we are as therapists, who we can work with, what we can tolerate and what remains beyond our limits even when we are at our most optimistic. [73, p.320]

A Final Comment or Two

We were interested in hearing the considered opinion of other people in our team and from the people sitting in the chair opposite us. We were surprised and encouraged by the level of care, thought and insight the people we'd attempted to treat responded with on being asked to give their perspectives. With more clarity than we could have predicted, they seem to have confirmed to us the validity of the principles of care and treatment outlined in this book. If Mara had been treated with anything other than careful respect, she would have left us in a second, feeling as though her sense of shame was entirely justified. If we'd not journeyed into difficult territory with Jade, stepping outside her psychosis, we would've simply exacerbated her avoidance of the aspects of her life she was trying to avoid.

Working with people with BPD can be complex, risky and stressful. There are so many factors involved in the application of our principles of treatment (whatever specific modality of treatment a team may adhere to) that there is always the chance even the best considered approach will not 'work' or that the outcomes at times may, at times, be modest. Despite this, more than anything, these examples confirm to us that the challenge of working with people with BPD is genuinely rewarding and, ultimately, hopeful.

Chapter 7

BEYOND THE BORDER

Just over a quarter of a century ago, Glyn Lewis and Louis Appleby published their paper 'Personality Disorder: The Patients Psychiatrists Dislike'. [74] In this study, a sample of psychiatrists perceived patients previously given a diagnosis of personality disorder as more difficult and less deserving of mental health services than patients with other diagnoses. The patients with personality disorder 'were seen as manipulative, difficult to manage, unlikely to arouse sympathy, annoying … uncompliant, not accepting advice, and having a poor prognosis'. [74, p.47] There was also a perception that people given this label rarely respond to treatment. The authors concluded their paper by stating that the label 'personality disorder' led to such pejorative judgments within mental health services that it should be scrapped.

Today, we believe there is a change in the wind, given the increasing focus on the biological differences between people who have and who do not have borderline personality disorder (BPD). The following excerpt from a journal article that I wrote with an Australian colleague and had published a few years back encapsulates our thinking in this regard:

> New diagnoses [in relation to BPD] will continue to expand as boundaries broaden. While awaiting revolutionary understanding in psychiatry, uncertainty will continue. The associated discomfort is being managed by imposing structures rather than by accepting the non-perfectibility of science, the medical practitioner or the patient. However, this latter acceptance allows a more gentle, humane and realistic approach to the clinical dilemma. Given that diagnostic certainty is not possible, maintaining a curious stance, 'What do they see that I am not yet able to see?' is important. Individual practitioner responses reflect a variety of biases, and when explicitly acknowledged, allow clinician and patient to develop a shared understanding. It is perhaps this respectful synchrony, an unhurried gentleness, that enables much work to be effectively undertaken. [4, p.307]

AN APPROACH SUITED TO UNCERTAINTY

The last sentence of the above excerpt was, in a way, prophetic of the approach we've been developing in recent years in our work with people who present with what experience and the literature tell us are the characteristics of BPD. It is this approach, of course, which has wound through the stories from the border presented in this book. 'Unhurried gentleness' and 'respectful synchrony' have coalesced into the principles and practice of taking time to observe and reflect, of exhibiting a humane understanding, and of having all members of the therapeutic team encourage patients to acknowledge and take some measure of self-responsibility and self-management with respect to their situation.

Unhurried gentleness encapsulates our premise that time is needed to understand just what *is* happening for the person who presents and what the characteristics of that presentation means in terms of diagnosis and treatment. Resisting the urge to make an immediate diagnosis of the person's presentation allows us to slow down and observe. It also, of course, lessens the chance of misdiagnosis. We can carefully review what others have said and noted about the person, take aboard the person's telling of their story as they see it, and then set that information against our own observations and eventual formulations.

Our admonition to take time acknowledges imprecision in psychiatric diagnoses. As Dr Edwin R Wallace IV observed, 'Psychiatry consumes and cross checks itself with the best available basis and clinical science; struggles for the most rigorous and self-reflective clinical judgement; applies it to the unique patient phenomenologically and empathically; and seeks more coherently comprehensive and evidenced, although always tentative and evolving, theories and formulation.' [75, p.300] For us, diagnosis in the field of psychiatry may be usefully considered as a hunch held lightly rather than a decision to be defended. Symptomatic responsivity is of interest, not of diagnostic confirmation. If we do not move cautiously before adopting a diagnosis uncritically, we diminish both psychiatry and the scientific method of observe, test, verify. Think Ptolemy, Copernicus, Galileo and Kepler with respect to our evolving understanding of the place of Earth in the universe.

While we wait for revolutionary understanding in psychiatry, we must entertain uncertainty and its associated discomfort. One way of managing that discomfort is to impose the structures of diagnostic certainty and associated treatments. Another is to accept fallibility in science, the mental health system, medical practitioners, the people we work with; in short, to accept that diagnostic certainty is currently not possible. We consider that acceptance brings a slower and thus gentler, more humane and realistic approach to gaining understanding of what is happening for the person. The approach invites us to exercise curiosity, to ask ourselves and the colleagues in our team such questions as the one in the quote cited above: 'What are others seeing in this person's presentation that I am not yet able to see?' Other questions might be:

Are my own clinical biases distorting my perceptions?

What are alternative possibilities?

What has been happening in the person's life that might explain why they are behaving as they are?

What has *just* happened to them to bring them to the attention of a mental health service?

Slowing down provides time for patient and therapist to build trust in one another and to identify and therefore overcome the dangers of transference and countertransference. It allows both to begin the type of conversation wherein the patient feels secure enough to begin telling their stories, to provide information about themselves that contributes to answers to the above questions. Answers to these questions, in turn, help us make decisions about whether medication, certain types of therapy, establishing boundaries (such as saying no, choosing not to rescue), changing some feature of the person's life (for example, setting up help in the home) or all of the above might be the way to proceed.

Humane understanding allows us to establish and maintain our connection with the person as a person even when they frustrate us, when we do not like them, when they reject our therapeutic overtures, when we struggle to find a way forward for them and ourselves. As long as we can maintain sight of, *feel* something for the person within the bundle of characteristics that form their presentation, we have a means of staying connected to them as people trying to cope with what has happened and is happening to them. Our ethos, essentially, is one of shared humanity—people *matter*. [8] As a colleague, Michaela Burt, who leads a low-secure mental health unit in the UK, emphasizes, 'Treat people as if they were what they ought to be, and you will help them become what they are capable of becoming.'

Her words have resonated for us while writing this book. For example, I recently read Mara's sections of the book to her and asked her what she took from them. I wasn't expecting her reply: 'That you believe in me.' A little while ago, Kate received a gift from Mara—a canvas filled with messages, one of which thanked Kate for believing in her when she felt lost. I now recall, having not 'heard' the words at the time, similar comments from others:

'You still wanted to see me.'

'You didn't give up.'

'You believed that I could do it.'

"You were willing to offer me sixteen weeks of therapy"

Until writing this book, I hadn't fully appreciated how important it is for our clients to be believed in as people as opposed to having them just believe in our approach.

Humane understanding also means recognizing our own human frailty as therapists, clinicians, practitioners. We do not always have the answers—or at least not immediate ones. Our fears, fatigues and frustrations can impede our work. We get it wrong, make errors. We take calculated risks. Sometimes we have to live with the knowledge that despite what we decided to do, or not do, as part of our therapeutic approach, the person chose to deal with their struggle by taking some action destructive to themselves and/or other people in their lives.

The building of trust that comes not only from taking time but also from exhibiting humane understanding helps us create a climate in which the person can begin to take self-responsibility. This means they can explicitly acknowledge their situation and their role in it, and from there commit to the work needed to ameliorate or resolve it. Self-responsibility allows for deeper, therapeutically useful conversations not only between the person and practitioners but also between the person and significant others in their life. It leads to the person and clinician developing a shared understanding of the person's presentation, a mutuality which enables the former to work in synchrony with the latter during the therapy, rather than being the passive recipient of treatment.

The Invitation to Dance

In our experience, *synchrony*, or to give it another name, collaboration, brings 'stickability' to therapy-based agreements, such as lessening reliance on a medication or not contacting, in the interest of the person exercising self-responsibility and self-management, the psychiatrist or other specified team members, outside scheduled meeting times. It also allows both parties to acknowledge that there may never be a full resolution to the person's struggle. In such instances, the work becomes one of acceptance that the point at which the person can go no further is the best they can do. This is equally true for the therapist.

Respectful synchrony for us also holds the meaning of the 'dance' between patient and therapist(s) that begins as an invitation. As I have written elsewhere, 'Diagnosis is an invitation to dance. Either party can offer, accept or decline the process, itself inviting conversation.' [4]

The notion that diagnosis is the point at which the invitation is extended does not mean the diagnosis is one that both parties agree on, let alone that is a valid one. A person can come to me or any other member of our team, either with a self-diagnosis or one given by another party. Equipped with that diagnosis, the person may request, sometimes demand, a certain course of treatment (often medication). That is their invitation to me to dance. But I can decline that invitation because I am not certain of or I disagree with the diagnosis and/or the treatment. I can then offer, sometimes stipulate (from my professional judgement), an alternative, which the person may accept, decline, resist. The dance continues until we both agree on what is happening for the person (the diagnosis) and the therapy. And so, as Duncan commented earlier in this book, the dance that is the generally the hard work of therapy begins. If trust is established during the early stages of the relationship between person and therapist, then it's likely to be partnered by respect—of each partner for the other. Hence, the dance becomes one of respectful synchrony.

This is not to suggest that the dance will be all fluid movement. There will likely be stumbling, missteps, mistiming, asynchronous rhythms. Trust may break down from time to time, and power differentials (perhaps acknowledged, perhaps not) between person and practitioner will manifest. There will be times when the person, the clinician and other members of the team find it hard to maintain a previously discussed and seemingly agreed on course of action. The person may continue phoning a clinic or turning up at it outside agreed meeting times. The therapist may not be able to resist the urge to rescue the person. In such instances, there may be responses in place for these contingencies, such as our 'holding the line' method in response to 'outside-agreed-times' contact. Whatever the event, there needs to be acknowledgement and acceptance of it; then, assuming the overall approach still seems the best course of action, a return to it.

FINAL THOUGHTS

While many ultimately useful interventions are derived from a thorough formulation of a person's difficulties, some are more serendipitous in their origins. This has been our experience in developing our approach to working with people with characteristics symptomatic of BPD. Formal training, observation, discussion with colleagues, different therapeutic methodologies, interpretation of relevant literature and teamwork have all fed into this approach. But it is our application of it over time with our clients that has allowed us to hone and gain confidence in it. As a team, it has been a case of feedback and feedforward as we discuss in regular meetings how and why aspects of our approach have worked or not worked, and what the implications are for our ongoing practice. Some of our most valuable learnings have come from serendipitous events, such as Duncan and Kate taking Mara to see *Star Trek*.

For all of us, particular aspects of our approach described in this book, such as saying no, holding the line, taking risks, not medicating as a matter of routine, are not easy. They're not easy for the people we work with either, of course. But our experience and the experiences and commentary of these people show that these features do have promise, and that they have, in fact, lived up to the promise. This is not to say that our approach or any one or more aspects of it always have the hoped for outcomes. It doesn't; they don't. Some patients will reject the whole approach, or aspects of it. Others will get a certain distance and be able to go no further. And some, or actually, as we have found, a good many, will break through and cross the border into a place where they've come to terms with past trauma and themselves. Having got beyond the border, they find themselves able to manage and to move on into a healthy and hopeful future.

Diversity of response to our approach signals the importance of not seeing it as prescription. Rather, it is a set of principles that informs various practices. Application of these practices should be guided by another principle, flexibility. Trite a reminder as some might perceive it, each person we work with is unique and so requires understandings and responses tailored to (and *with*) them and their circumstances. Similarly, each of us working in our teams brings different strengths and skills to our practice in general and our application of our approach in particular.

Thus, Duncan, for example, is technically skilled and able to offer a range of specific interventions tailored to the individual and carefully titrated to their rate of change. My emphasis has been to rely on the person being able and interested to understand, discover, and change themselves as responsible, competent adults. Today, my questions to the person invariably return to: 'How did you do that [e.g., self-manage a challenge]?' 'What did you do differently [e.g., from what you had done before that allowed you to cope]?'

Kate reminds us that it is essential that the person recognizes and rehearses those means by which they can manage their distress before they can move into real and confronting therapy. All of us remain attached to the idea of being clear with people that they have an opportunity to interact differently. We've been encouraged by how helpful this approach has been for our team and for others (family, friends, health and social services) with whom the person has contact.

Flexibility gains more cogency if our supposition that the borderline experience will continue to change is verified. We started this book with the intention of writing about people we have worked with during our practice who met the criteria for BPD. As we finish it, we are less certain. Telling the stories in this book and reflecting on them has led us to think that people, typically presenting to psychiatric services in ways that are initially alarming and bewildering, are actually managing the best way they know how given what has happened to them.

POSTSCRIPT

We began this book with a story of an old Chinese woman carrying a cracked pot. All of us, like the cracked pot, wonder whether we can do better: the people who we see and who struggle as a result of what has happened to them, and ourselves as therapists when we can't do what we hoped we might do and when we don't behave in ways we know we ideally should.

I've just met three new women (new to our clinic that is). One knows deep down that she doesn't have an illness and is pleased to have her instinct confirmed. Her story, what had happened to her and how she adapted in order to survive, is sufficient explanation for the thoughts, feelings and behaviour which had alarmed and bewildered her. The second woman is less certain. It seems to me that she still wishes to cling to her medication in the same way that she wants to cling to a mother who was never there for her. The third is still courting with her various adventures and isn't ready to give those up just yet. I have, however, been able to be clear with all there. 'I'm biased,' I begin. 'I'm not much of a diagnosis or medication sort of person. I wonder whether we might think about this a little differently.'

Duncan, whose clarity and good humour reminds me when I start to drift from our principles, the people who've given their stories, and the process of writing have all refined my practice. Just as the water from the Chinese woman's cracked pot was a gift to the plants, the gifts have been plentiful and frequently unexpected. We hope the stories from the border and beyond told in this book offer someone the same. For us, people's kindness and willingness to share their stories in the hope of benefiting others has been and remains the most cogent and humbling experience of producing it.

We also hope we've made clear in this book just how vital we think a unified approach from the whole team is in terms of enabling people with borderline personality disorder to understand their story, make peace with their emotions and to know they are capable of changing their own lives.

It's now Friday 5 p.m. My wife and I are getting up at 3 a.m. tomorrow to catch an early morning flight to see our son. The girls are already en route and Alex leaves later today. We're all going to meet up, to be together. When we get back, our fax machine will have been replaced with email!

REFERENCES

These references, along with the suggested further reading that follows, provide a body of work that collect in one place our thoughts, ideas and experiences over our professional lives—at least to date! We've annotated some of the references that we consider particularly useful in terms of the ideas discussed in this book.

[1] Little J, Rouhan J. An organisational and community-based approach to deliberate self harm. *Australasian Psychiatry* 2009;17: 169–170.

[2] Ballarat Health Services, Grampian Psychiatric Services. Caring in a different way: An organisational and community-based approach to deliberate self harm. Ballarat, Australia: Ballarat Health Services; 1999. These are the course notes for a two-day workshop that we ran.

[3] Little JD, Bipolar II and the birth of a new physics. *Australia & New Zealand Journal of Psychiatry* 2013;47: 882. It took 1200 years for Copernicus's notion that the sun, not Earth, was at the centre of the universe. However, with sincerity, interest in broadening the bipolar spectrum may be premature.

[4] Little J, Richardson K. The clinician's dilemma: Borderline personality disorder or bipolar spectrum disorder? *Australasian Psychiatry* 2010;18(5): 303–308. Examines subjectivity in the diagnostic process, acknowledging the role of bias and the limitation of the scientific method. A theoretical paper.

[5] Paris J. Borderline or bipolar? Distinguishing borderline personality disorder from bipolar spectrum disorders. *Harvard Review Psychiatry* 2004;12: 140–145. doi: 10.4088/JCP.13m08428

[6] Akisakal HGS, Djerderedjian AH, Rosenthal RH, Khani MK. Cyclothymic disorder: Bipolar spectrum disorders. *Harvard Review Psychiatry* 2004;12: 140–145.

[7] Toulmin S. Agent and patient in psychiatry. *International Journal of Law and Psychiatry* 1980;3: 267–268. Surprisingly helpful.

[8] Mill JS. *Three essays: On liberty, representative government, the subjection of women*. Oxford, UK: Oxford University Press; 1975.

[9] Little, J. Do I matter? Therapeutic communities. *The International Journal of Therapeutic Communities* 2014;35(1): 1–4. doi: 10.1108/TC-03-2013-0004. The point is in the title. I often ask the people I work with this question.

[10] Watts D, Morgan, G. Malignant alienation. *British Journal of Psychiatry* 1994;164: 11–15. This paper is a useful reminder of what can happen when people feel they matter to no one.

[11] Murphy GE, Guze SP. Setting limits: The management of the manipulative patient. *American Journal of Psychotherapy* 1960;14: 30–47. Written over 50 years ago and still a classic.

[12] Abroms GM Setting limits. *Archives of General Psychology* 1968;19(1): 113–119.

[13] Phillips A. *Saying no: Why it's important for you and your child.* London, UK: Faber and Faber; 1999. A great read on an important topic. Well written and sensible.

[14] Little J. The therapeutic use of 'no'. Paper presented at the 13th International Congress on the Disorders of Personality, 16–19 September 2013, Copenhagen, Denmark. This paper provides a useful summary of the sparse literature on this very important topic.

[15] McCarthy JJ, Borders OT. Limit setting on drug abuse in methadone maintenance patients. *American Journal of Psychiatry* 1985;142(12): 1419–1423. This is the reference for the study showing better outcomes for people who were given a clear message.

[16] Orentlicher, D. Denying treatment to the non-compliant patient. *The Journal of the American Medical Association* 1991;265(12): 1579–1582. doi:10.1001/jama.1991.03460120093043. The original reference on Brenda Payton and the experience of the renal team.

[17] Stitzer ML, Petry, N, Silverman K. Contingency management therapies. In Strain EC, Stitzer ML (eds.) *The treatment of opioid dependence.* Baltimore, MD: The Johns Hopkins University Press; 2006, pp. 151–177.

[18] Bowlby J. *A secure base: parent–child attachment and healthy human development.* London, UK: Routledge; 1988.

[19] Ainsworth, MDS, Blehar, MC, Walters, E, Wall, S. Patterns of attachment: A psychological study of the strange situation. Hillsdale, NJ: Lawrence Erlbaum Associates; 1978.

[20] Kübler-Ross E. *On death and dying*. New York: Scribner; 1969. A classic.

[21] Axelman M. On holding the situation: Parental affect tolerance, limit setting, and the transition to object usage. *Journal of Infant, Child, and Adolescent Psychotherapy* 2009;8(2): 96–103. doi: 10.1080/15289160902949769.

[22] Bellinson J. You can't do that—or can you? Historical and clinical perspectives on limit setting in child psychotherapy. *Journal of Infant, Child, and Adolescent Psychotherapy* 2009;8(2); 87–95. doi: 10.1080/15289160902949678.

[23] Ehrensaft D. Discussion: Tightening up and lightening up. *Journal of Infant, Child, and Adolescent Psychotherapy* 2009;*8*(2): 104–112. doi: 10.1080/15289160902949744. doi:10.1080/15289160902949744

[24] Casement P. The setting of limits: A belief in growth. *Journal of Social Work Practice* 1992;6(1): 25–30. doi: 10.1080/02650539208413482.

[25] Basescu S. The threat of suicide in psychotherapy. *American Journal of Psychotherapy* 1965;19: 99–105.

[26] Maltsberger JT Calculated risks in the treatment of intractably suicidal patients. *Psychiatry: Interpersonal and Biological Processes* 1994;57: 199–212.

[27] Schwartz DA, Flinn DE, Slawson PF. Treatment of the suicidal character. *American Journal of Psychotherapy* 1974;28: 197–207.

[28] Straker G, Waks B. Limit setting in regard to self-damaging acts: The patient's perspective. *Psychotherapy: Theory, Research, Practice, Training* 1997;34(2):192–200. doi: 10.1037/h0087846.

[29] Waska R. Barely here to begin with and not-so-goodbyes: Keeping the faith when working with turbulent patients. *American Journal of Psychotherapy* 2012;66(1): 23–44.

[30] Green SA, Goldberg RL, Goldstein DM, Liebenluft E. *Limit setting in clinical practice.* Washington DC: American Psychiatric Press; 1988.

[31] Pam, A. Limit setting: Theory, techniques and risks. *American Journal of Psychotherapy* 1994;8(3): 432.

[32] Little J, Little B. Borderline personality disorder: Exceptions to the concept of responsible and competent. *Australasian Psychiatry* 2010;18(5): 445–450. Influenced by Dawson and MacMillan's approach wherein the person with borderline personality disorder is regarded as a responsible and competent adult, we examined whether neurocognitive differences or age constituted exceptions to the rule. We concluded they did not.

[33] Dawson D, MacMillan HL. *Relationship management of the borderline patient.* New York: Brunner/Mazel; 1993. This book is excellent. It is easy to read and paints a philosophy that we believe in, namely that the patient is respected as a competent, responsible adult, and provides really useful responses to awkward questions that you wished you'd thought of. If you're short of time, just focus on the middle sections, Chapters 5–8.

[34] Linehan quoted in Behnke SH, Saks ER. *Therapeutic jurisprudence: Informal consent as a clinical indicator for the chronically suicidal patient with borderline personality disorder. Loyola of Los Angeles Law Review* 1998;31: 945–982.

[35] Gutheil, T. Medicolegal pitfalls in the treatment of borderline patients. *American Journal of Psychiatry* 1985;142(1): 9–14. An excellent paper that should be read by all clinicians concerned about medico-legal aspects of care.

[36] Commonwealth of Australia. *Review of the law of negligence: Final report* (the IPP Report). Canberra, Australia: Commonwealth of Australia; 2002.

[37] Kernberg cited in Paris J. Managing suicidal crises in patients with severe personality disorders. In: van Luyn B, Akhtar S, Livesley WJ (eds.) *Severe personality disorders.* Cambridge, UK: Cambridge University Press; 2007, pp. 109–117. The actual sentence reads: 'Kernberg (1987) suggests that chronic suicidality requires patience rather than action' (p. 113).

[38] Landsberger HA. *Hawthorne revisited.* Ithaca, NY: Cornell University; 1958.

[39] Kennard D, Haigh R. Therapeutic communities. In: M Gelder (ed.) *The new Oxford textbook of psychiatry.* Oxford, UK: Oxford University Press, 2007; pp. 142–148.

[40] Sharrock J, Rickard, N. Limit setting: A useful strategy in rehabilitation. *Australian Journal of Advanced Nursing* 2002;19(4), 21–26.

[41] Group for the Advancement of Psychiatry. *Forced into treatment: The role of coercion in clinical practice* (Formulated by the Committee on Government Policy, Report no. 137). Arlington, VA: American Psychiatric Publishing; 1994.

[42] Landreth GL. Therapeutic limit setting in the play therapy relationship. *Professional Psychology: Research and Practice* 2002;33(6): 529–535. doi:10.1037/0735-7028.33.6.529.

[43] Siefert CJ (2012). A goal-oriented limited-duration approach for borderline personality disorder during brief inpatient hospitalizations. *Psychotherapy: Theory, Research, Practice, Training* 2012;49(4): 502–518. doi: 10.1037/a0026128.

[44] Goldberg RL. Psychodynamics of limit setting with the borderline patient. *The American Journal of Psychoanalysis* 1983;43(1): 71–75. doi: 10.1007/BF01253500.

[45] Shapiro E. The holding environment and family therapy with acting out adolescents. *International Journal of Psychoanalytic Psychiatrists* 1982;9: 202–226.

[46] Shabad P. Beyond determination and self-blame: The freedom to choose oneself. *Contemporary Psychoanalysis* 2007;43(2): 587–604. doi:10.1080/00107530.2007.10745935

[47] Little J, Little M, Little R. Rescuing: A universal phenomenon [in press]. *Australasian Psychiatry*. We were intrigued by the difficulty people have with respect to allowing their children to grow and assume the responsibilities of adulthood. The literature we reviewed enabled us to understand the genuine difficulties.

[48] Palmer, B. *Bipolar, borderline or both? Diagnostic/formulation issues in mood and personality disorders*. [Video] 2014. Available from https://www.youtube.com/watch?v =NcEAAZi3Qk0 [Accessed 16 August 2014].

[49] Svabado E. Kings and queens of chaos. *Psychology Today* 2013;46(5): 78.

[50] Distel MA, Rebollo-Mesa I, Willemsen G, Derom CA, Trull TJ, Martin, NG, et al. Familial resemblance of borderline personality disorder features: Genetic or cultural transmission? *PLoS ONE* 2009; 4(4): e5334. doi:10.1371/journal.pone.0005334

[51] Kendler KS, Myers J, Reichborn-Kjennerud T. Borderline personality disorder traits and their relationship with dimensions of normative personality: A web-based cohort and twin study *Acta Psychiatrica Scandanavica* 2011;123(5): 349–359.

[52] Gunderson, JG, Zanarini MC, Choi-Kain, LW, Mitchell, KS, Lang, KL, Hudson, JI. Family study of borderline personality disorder and its sectors of psychopathology. *Archives of General Psychiatry* 2011;68(7): 753–762. Not an inviting title but the evidence base for the relatively recent discovery that there is a high heritability associated with borderline personality disorder. Anything of John Gunderson's work is worth reading.

[53] Monterosso J, Royzman EB, Schwartz B. Explaining away responsibility: Effects of scientific explanation on perceived culpability. *Ethics and Behavior* 2005;15(2):139–158. Those clever psychologists!

[54] Astley R. Multiple metaphyseal fractures in small children (metaphyseal fragility of bone). *British Journal of Radiology* 1953;26(311): 577–583.

[55] Little J. Borderline personality disorder, neuroscience and responsibility. *Australian & New Zealand Journal of Psychiatry* 2014;48: 878. An attempt to summarise thoughts succinctly in relation to responsibility and the emerging biological emphasis appearing in the literature.

[56] Little, J. The prescription [in press]. *Australasian Psychiatry*. An attempt to succinctly summarize the multiple roles embedded within a prescription irrespective of the pharmacology. The letter also invites the clinician to consider any intervention, including hospitalisation and the allocation of case managers, as a prescription, and potentially with side-effects.

[57] Gutheil TG. The psychology of psychopharmacology. *Bulletin of the Menninger Clinic* 1982;46(4): 321–330. Gutheil's work is always thoughtful. This article is no exception.

[58] Stanley B, Siever LJ. The interpersonal dimension of borderline personality disorder: Toward a neuropeptide model. *American Journal of Psychiatry* 2010;167(1): 24–39. doi:10.1176/appi.ajp.2009.09050744. Current psychotropic medication is modest in its effectiveness at best. Larry Siever has been instrumental in examining in particular the biological correlates of impulsivity and the possible role of the opioids, oxytocin and vasopressin.

[59] Irwin S. How to prescribe psychoactive drugs. *Bulletin of the Menninger Clinic* 1974;38: 1–13.

[60] National Health and Medical Research Council. *Clinical practice guidelines for the management of borderline personality disorder*. Melbourne, Australia: National Health and Medical Research Council, Commonwealth of Australia; 2012.

[61] Carter A, Hall WD. The need for more explanatory humility in addiction neurobiology. *Addiction (Abingdon, England)* 2010;105(5), 790–791, 795–796. doi:10.1111/j.1360-0443.2009.02783.x.

[62] Little J, Stevens D. A patient-based voucher system for brief hospitalisation. *Australian & New Zealand Journal of Psychiatry* 1999;33: 429–432. The model we used to explain the development of this approach was locus of control. It seemed to work.

[63] Glannon W. Our brains are not us. *Bioethics* 2009;23(6), 321–329. doi: 10.1111/j.1467-8519.2009.01727.x.

[64] Morse SJ. Criminal responsibility and the disappearing person. *Cardozo Law Review* 2006;28(6): 2545–2575.

[65] Vincent NA. *Neuroscience and Legal Responsibility*. Oxford, UK: Oxford University Press; 2013.

[66] Rothschild B. *The body remembers: The psychophysiology of trauma and trauma treatment*. New York: WW Norton; 2007.

[67] van der Hart O, Nijenhuis ERS, Steele, K. *The haunted self: Structural dissociation and the treatment of chronic traumatization* (Norton Series on Interpersonal Neurobiology). New York, WW Norton; 2006.

[68] Flewett T. *Clinical risk management: An introductory text for mental health professionals*. Chatswood, Australia: Elsevier Australia; 2010.

[69] Tartaglia M, Little J. Clockwatching and hate [in press]. *Australasian Psychiatry*. Despite Michael entering practice and me retiring, the themes remain and are usefully thought and talked about rather than ignored.

[70] Gabbard GO, Wilkinson SM. *Management of countertransference with borderline patients*. Gabbard GO: American Psychiatric Press; 1994.

[71] Maltsberger JT, Buie DH. Countertransference: Hate in the treatment of suicidal patients. *Archives General Psychiatry* 1974;30(5): 625–633.

[72] Roberts VZ. The self-assigned impossible task. In: Obholzer A, Roberts VZ (eds.) The unconscious at work: Individual and organisational stress in the human services. London, UK: Routledge; 1994, pp.110–120.

[73] Brown G, Kainth K, Matheson C, Osborne J, Trenkle A, Adlam J. An hospitable engagement? Open-door psychotherapy with the socially excluded. *Psychodynamic Practice* 2011;17(3): 307–324.

[74] Lewis G, Appelby L. *British Journal of Psychiatry* 1988;153: 44–49.

[75] Wallace ER. Psychiatry and its nosology: In: Sadler JZ, Wiggins OP, Schwartz MA (eds.) *Philosophical perspectives on psychiatric diagnostic classification.* Baltimore, MD: The Johns Hopkins University Press, 1994; pp. 295–314.

Further Reading

Salter AC. Predators. New York: Basic Books: 2003. I sought out this little book having seen one of Ann Salter's video interviews. She had spent more than 20 years sitting with sex offenders, who, having been convicted and sentenced, knew they could no longer be hurt legally. We wanted to put this up front, hoping that readers, distracted by the other references, might read this one, the following quote being chilling: 'They tell me how they operate and how they got away with assaults for so long. They tell me how they make assessments of people like you and me.' This is an extraordinary account of how the predator is never seen or considered, for we have invited them into our home. It is why we don't use male babysitters.

Berwick D. Disseminating innovations in healthcare. *The Journal of the American Medical Association* 2003; 289(15): 1969–1975. Nice description and valuing of both early and late adopters to change.

Cramer MA. Under the influence of unconscious process: Countertransference in the treatment of PTSD and substance abuse in women. *American Journal of Psychotherapy* 2002;56(2): 194–210. I came across this article recently and shared it with the team. It comes from a regular tutorial series run by Melbourne-based Dr Ed Harari and is superb.

Draper H, Sorell T. Patients' responsibilities in medical ethics. *Bioethics* 2002;16(4): 335–352. doi: 10.1111/1467-8519.00292. An uncommon topic, namely that ethical responsibility is bidirectional. Reassuring, but a little blunt in places.

Greenberg LS. *Emotion-focused therapy*. New York: John Wiley & Sons; 2004.

Kezelman C, Stavropoulis P. *The last frontier: Practice guidelines for treatment of complex trauma and trauma informed care and service delivery*. Kirribilli, Australia: Adults Surviving Child Abuse (ASCA); 2012.

Koekkoek, B, van Meijil, B, Hutschemaekers, G. Difficult patients in mental health care: A review. *Psychiatric Services* 2006;57(6): 795–802.

Krawitz R, Watson C. *Borderline personality disorder: A practical guide to treatment.* Oxford, UK: Oxford University Press; 2003. This excellent little book looks at the practicalities of treatment.

Linehan MM. *Cognitive-behavioral treatment of borderline personality disorder*. New York, Guilford Press; 1993.

Little J, Blackman P, Rouhan J. Social policy and humanity: The use of language as a social defence against anxiety. *Australasian Psychiatry* 2001;9(4): 317–320. doi: 10.1046/j.1440-1665.2001.00357.x.

Little J, Trauer T, Rouhan J, Haines M. Borderline personality disorder and interagency response. *Australasian Psychiatry* 2010;18(5): 441–444. doi: 10.3109/10398562.2010.498886. This was a summary of a year's worth of work. It included visits and talks across a huge area of Australia, as well as a questionnaire designed to collect information on various professions' understanding of borderline personality disorder.

Mulder R. Problems with suicide risk assessments. *Australian & NZ Journal of Psychiatry* 2011;45(8): 605–607.

Plakun EM (ed.) *Treatment resistance and patient authority: The Austen Riggs reader*. New York: WW Norton; 2011.

Pryor, K. *Don't shoot the dog! The new art of teaching and training*. Lydney, UK: Ringpress Books; 2006.

Scanlon C, Adlam J. Refusal, social exclusion and the cycle of rejection: A cynical analysis. *Critical Social Policy* 2008;28(4): 929–949. doi: 10.1177/0261018308095301.

Smoller JW. The etiology and treatment of childhood. In: Ellenbogen, GC (ed.) *Oral sadism and the vegetarian personality*. New York: Bruner/Mazel;1987, p. 5–12. Although the approach is light-hearted, describing normal childhood through the lens of a diagnostic process highlights the inherent errors of unquestioned observation.

Stern S. The conundrum of self-care. *Contemporary Psychoanalysis* 2007;43(4): 605–620.

Stobbe E. Psychiatry discriminates against people with borderline personality disorder. *BrainBlogger*. Weblog [Online]. Available from: http://brainblogger.com/2006/06/20/anti-stigmatization-psychiatry-discriminates-against-people-with-borderline-personality-disorder/ [Accessed 18 August 2014].

Swoskin MH. Psychoanalysis and medication. *Bulletin of the Menninger Clinic* 2001;65: 143–159.

Weick KE. Tool retention and fatalities in wildland fire setting. In: Salas E, Klein G (eds.) *Linking expertise and naturalist decision making*. Mahwah, NJ: Lawrence Erlbaum Associates; 2001, pp. 321–326.

Winer JA, Andriukaitis, SM. Interpersonal aspects of initiating pharmacotherapy. *Psychiatric Annals* 1989;19: 318–323.

Yalom ID. *Love's executioner and other tales of psychotherapy*. New York: Basic Books; 2012.

INDEX

C

D

G

H

I

T

U

V

W

Y